WAVES OF BLISS

WAVES OF BLISS

Sri Swami Sivananda

Published by

THE DIVINE LIFE SOCIETY
P.O. SHIVANANDANAGAR—249 192
Distt. Tehri-Garhwal, Uttaranchal, Himalayas, India
www.sivanandaonline.org, www.dlshq.org

WAVES OF BLISS

Sri Swami Sivananda

Published by

THE DIVINE LIFE SOCIETY
P.O. SHIVANANDANAGAR—249 192
Distt. Tehri-Garhwal, Uttaranchal, Himalayas, India
www.sivanandaonline.org, www.dlshq.org

First Edition: 1949
Second Edition: 2007
Third Edition: 2013
[1,000 Copies]

©The Divine Life Trust Society

ISBN 81-7052-193-9
ES 18

PRICE: ₹75/-

Published by Swami Padmanabhananda for
The Divine Life Society, Shivanandanagar, and printed
by him at the Yoga-Vedanta Forest Academy Press,
P.O. Shivanandanagar, Distt. Tehri-Garhwal,
Uttaranchal, Himalayas, India
For online orders and Catalogue visit : dlsbooks.org

OM
Dedicated
to the
Busy Aspirant
Who Needs
Spiritual Truths
in
Easily Assimilable Vitamin-Capsules

ॐ

1st January 1950

Beloved Jignasus,

'Waves of Bliss' is a spiritual tonic. It is a sure panacea for the disease of birth & death. It contains the Secret of Sadhana. It is your constant companion, preceptor and spiritual benefactor.

It will be the Solace of your life. It will elevate and inspire you. Take a dip and come out enlightened.

Sivananda

SRI SWAMI SIVANANDA

Born on the 8th September, 1887, in the illustrious family of Sage Appayya Dikshitar and several other renowned saints and savants, Sri Swami Sivananda had a natural flair for a life devoted to the study and practice of Vedanta. Added to this was an inborn eagerness to serve all and an innate feeling of unity with all mankind.

His passion for service drew him to the medical career; and soon he gravitated to where he thought that his service was most needed. Malaya claimed him. He had earlier been editing a health journal and wrote extensively on health problems. He discovered that people needed right knowledge most of all; dissemination of that knowledge he espoused as his own mission.

It was divine dispensation and the blessing of God upon mankind that the doctor of body and mind renounced his career and took to a life of renunciation to qualify for ministering to the soul of man. He settled down at Rishikesh in 1924, practised intense austerities and shone as a great Yogi, saint, sage and Jivanmukta.

In 1932 Swami Sivananda started the Sivanandashram. In 1936 was born The Divine Life Society. In 1948 the Yoga-Vedanta Forest Academy was organised. Dissemination of spiritual knowledge and training of people in Yoga and Vedanta were their aim and object. In 1950 Swamiji undertook a lightning tour of India and Ceylon. In 1953 Swamiji convened a 'World Parliament of Religions'. Swamiji is the author of over 300 volumes and has disciples all over the world, belonging to all nationalities, religions and creeds. To read Swamiji's works is to drink at the Fountain of Wisdom Supreme. On 14th July, 1963 Swamiji entered Mahasamadhi.

PREFACE

Spiritual knowledge is imparted with the best result not through the precision of logic and reason, but through image, literature, art and beauty. It is the change of the feelings heart and not the understandings of the brain that touches the being of the inner man. Adhyatma-Vidya is the science of the innermost essence of the universe and it cannot therefore, come under the intellectual categories of objective discernment. The teachings of the sages have all had the conspicuous characteristic of appealing to the whole nature of the human being,—not merely an aspect of him. The highest teachings are executed in the homely language, the language of the heart of man. The simple great declarations of the Upanishads serve as examples.

We have here the Waves of Bliss, the materialisation of the spontaneous flow out of the depth of Swami Sivananda. It is a book meant for children and adults, the young and the old, men and women alike. The human touch in him coupled with his deep sagacity and impervious knowledge have proved to be such a beautiful combination of the relative and the superphysical characters that his writings are a joy to the sorrowful, a strength to the weak, an illumination to the ignorant. The blending of intelligence and feeling, a melting of the head and the heart, is a common feature found in these outflows of his blissful expressions. Human troubles are not alleviated through flowery speeches and subtle hairsplitting, for the source of sorrow is rooted in the very make-up of the individual and not in his superficial coatings. The inner disease is not cured by washing the outer shirt. The root has to be dug out.

A study of these highly spiritual lines from the holy pen of the saint is meant to cheer up the weary aspirant in his journey towards the City of the Immortal. These Waves shall bathe all with the Peace of Bliss, and everyone shall return elevated to the height of the joy of the Real is our fervent hope.

—SWAMI CHIDANANDA

INTRODUCTION

The "Waves of Bliss" here presented are the pointers to the "Waves of Bliss" of the Atman, Purusha or Brahman. The Supreme Attainment is of the Truth which is Existence, Knowledge and Bliss Absolute.

Man begins from his physical body and ends in the spiritual Soul. He lives in his external expressions whereas in reality, he is the all-pervading Self. Hence his march is from the external to the internal, from the apparent to the True, from the shadow to the Light, from the perishable to the Immortal.

The path to perfection lies through the regulated discipline of every such materialisation of the Self—body, mind and spirit. If any one is neglected, that shall speak in a loud voice and disturb the peace of spiritual Sadhana. He is a true Sadhaka who has known that the body is mind-appearing, that the mind is the Atman appearing, that the Atman is identical with the Absolute, and that hence, Sadhana is the same process of inner transformation which aims to integrate the scattered self-findings in the form of the world phenomena, into the One Consciousness of the Infinite. The body should be taken care of. The mind should be controlled. The Self should be realised. An aspirant has to adjust his dealings with these layers of the different degrees of reality with severe discrimination.

Right discrimination points to the existence of a permanent Being which is untouched by the passing appearances. That is God, Truth or Brahman. The first section of this book deals with this eternal background of the universe. This Reality does not only pervade but is the very existence of all that can ever be. Only It exists in essence. Nothing second to It can ever exist. That is to be known. That is to be realised.

Discrimination, again, detects the impermanent and false character of the universe. The Second Chapter is devoted to this subject. The highest fulfilment is the effect of the greatest renunciation. All beings die whether they wish it or not. The supremacy of death seems to be unquestionable. Mundane objects give rise to bitter experiences in life. The will to live is a terrible pest and enjoyments in life are harbingers of extreme misery. The body is a prison and Maya is ever deluding. Real renunciation is overcoming the sense of egoism.

Man is steeped in ignorance. The Third Chapter is an exhortation to the human being in general to wake up from his nescience. The blows which are received from the world should make one disgusted with worldly life in toto. There is no need to bewail. Man is Divine in his essential nature. He must search out this centre of eternity buried in his core. Life in family is not happy. Power, name and fame are phantasms. The life of a Jivanmukta is the most blessed. He who is immersed in the bliss of Brahman alone is happy. Man's life is meant to prepare him for this existence supreme. The life led by the people of the world is in every way artificial, undivine and against the nature of the Reality. The whole world is a scene of the play of the not-Self, of Maya, of delusion. Conceit and vanity reign supreme in all men. Crookedness and cunningness have slaughtered the glorious infinitude of man's nature. The salvation of the worldly individual lies through the sacrifice of his brute investiture and surrendering himself to the Eternal Being.

The aspirant's conduct in relation to his Guru and the method of Sadhana are expounded in the next three sections. Sadhana should be integral and not lop-sided. The keynote of spiritual practice is inhibition of the mind, renunciation of the self, expansion of consciousness. Self-realisation is not a joke; it is a hard job. It requires complete self-abnegation and clinging to the Life Eternal. A fiery determination attended with clear understanding of the pros and cons of the way of self-unfoldment and illumination is required of every true aspirant. Ethical perfection is the foundation for the building of the superstructure of Truth-Consciousness. Yama, Niyama and Sadhana Chatushtaya are the most important prerequisites of all modes of Sadhana. These moral laws are categorical imperatives. They can be excluded by none.

False imagination has bound the Jivas to their limited vision of life. Death shall run away from him who has opened his eye of the spiritual light within. This opening of consciousness is possible through the negation of the psychological cloggings in the form of "I"-ness and "Mine"-ness, which dangerous habits spare none on earth. Only the sage or the Viveki is free from these erroneous conceptions.

The highest wisdom is hidden in one's own being. Only a finding out of this fact is the goal of all Sadhana. Sadhana is not a traditional rule laid down as eternal for all individuals, but its methods change themselves according to the temperaments, conditions and requirements of the aspirant. All irrational fads have to be cast away and pet dogmas transcended in order to be open to the revelation of the differenceless and unlimited Absolute.

Devotion to God is the individualised love of the heart centred in cosmic existence. It is a disintegration of particularised affection into universal joy. The feeling of love is involuntary in the human being. He must but love something. His bondage lies in the pitiable fact that his love is directed to objects defined by space and time. He is saved when his emotion is lifted up from individual attachment to the Absolute Attachment. The devotee is not expected to conceive of God as limited by space, for God is infinite. A personal God is necessary in the beginning but He is not a perfect God, for personality is limitation. Hence God is the universal essence unlimited and utterly perfect. Such a devotee is freed from the bonds of sin and action. He is helped by the divine hand in every stage of his life. The Eighth Chapter has its purport in the love of God and complete surrender to His Will, for the sake of the self's salvation.

Such a life of strenuous self-discipline opens the bud of the soul which blossoms into the transcendental height of absolute experience arrived at through integrated meditations as enumerated in the later chapters. The dehypnotisation of the self from its belief in the world and the individual into the consciousness of the Absolute is effected through positive affirmations of one's being the Infinite Consciousness and Bliss of Immortality and Eternity. The methods are highly advanced and can be practised easily by those who have dedicated themselves to the cause of the Realisation of the Infinite. Even a slight tinge of worldliness makes one unfit for experiencing such an exalted condition of the Truth of Brahman. Truth does not allow even the feeblest air of the entrance of relativity into it. The boldest aspirant jumps into this infinite abyss and seeks to dissolve himself in its bosom of undying bliss.

These Waves of Bliss shall lose themselves in the Ocean of Bliss and take him also with them who is caught in their current.

PRAYER

Prostrations to Lord Siva, who is the Supreme Guru, who is an embodiment of Eternal Life, Knowledge and Bliss, who is free from worldliness, who is an embodiment of Peace, who is without any support and who is Light of lights.

Brethren! Meet together; talk together; let your minds apprehend alike; common be your prayer; common be your assembly's end and aim; common be your purpose; common be your deliberation; I advise you to have a common policy. Common be your desires; united be your hearts; united be your intention, so that there may be a thorough union among you. May our Father grant this.

May there be welfare to the whole world! May all beings devote themselves to doing good to others! May all evils subside! May the world be happy in all ways!

WISDOM NECTAR

Goal of life is Self-Realisation.
Freedom is thy birthright.
Time is fleeting.
Thou art a pilgrim here.
Your everlasting abode is Brahman.
Live in God (Atman).
Brahmacharya is Divine Life.
Practise Ahimsa, Satyam, Brahmacharya.
Service is worship.
Serve. Love. Give.
Serve the poor and the sick.
Be good. Do good. Be kind. Be pure.
Brahman is real. World is unreal.
Hear. Reflect. Meditate. Realise.
Enquire: "Who am I?"
Know thyself and be free.
"Tat Tvam Asi"—That thou art.
Realise this and be free.

Note:—Remember the above lines daily. Print or write each line in separate post card in bold types and fix them in prominent places in your house. These lines will inspire you to lead a Divine Life. You will not be carried away by worldly temptations.

THE DIVINE LIFE

Man has forgotten his inherent nature on account of ignorance and so he is tossed about hither and thither in the ocean of this Samsara by the two currents of Raga and Dvesha—like and dislike. He is not leading the Divine Life and therefore he has become a slave of his senses, passion and impulses. He vainly searches for his happiness in perishable objects that are conditioned in time, space and causation and therefore he has no peace of mind. The musk deer does not know that the fragrance of musk is emanating from its own navel. It wanders about here and there to find out the source of this smell. Evan so, the deluded ignorant man is not aware of the fountain of bliss within himself in the immortal Atman or soul and he is running after the external perishable objects to get happiness.

You can have permanent peace if you turn your mind from the objective universe and live in the divine within your heart. You can be free from cares, worries, anxieties, fear, delusion, doubt, etc., only if you lead a Divine Life by getting purity of heart and concentration of mind. Divine Life is not possible without purity of heart. Concentration, meditation and communion, are not attainable without Chitta Suddhi, through constant and protracted selfless service.

People are thirsting for spiritual ideas, contact with evolved souls. The materialistic West also is tired of money and power. They do not find any solace here. They are directing slowly their attention towards the quest of God and search of Mahatmas. They visit India in search of Satgurus and Yogins.

Blessed is he who is tired of this tormenting, degenerating materialistic life and who longs to lead a divine life; twice blessed is he who has dispassion and discrimination, who goes to Mahatmas to have Satsanga, and gets advice and tries to lead a Divine Life; thrice blessed is he who lives in God always, who feels the Divine Presence everywhere, in every face, in every motion, in every feeling, in every sentiment and in every atom or electron.

May the blessings of sages, Rishis and Yogis be upon you all!

UNIVERSAL PRAYER

O adorable Lord of the Universe!
    Salutations and prostrations unto Thee.

Thou art the only refuge of all beings,
    Thou art the Bestower of Immortality.

Thou art the Father, Mother and Guide,
    Thou art the support and source of all;
    Shower Thy grace on me.

Deliver me from evils and temptations;
    I come to Thee, my sole Refuge.

Abandoning all attachments to the world,
    Yearning for liberation,

Extinction of my self and merging into Thee
    The Support and Source of all.

THE UNIVERSAL ANTHEM—I

(Thars: Rama Hare Siya Rama Ram)

Glory to Thee, O fair Mother Earth,
    Common Parent thou of all Humanity.
The common sacred place of birth,
    Of entire Mankind so vast and mighty.

Bless thou O Mother, bless one and all,
    All Thy children in colour black or white,
Brown or even yellow, short or tall,
    To feel and to bask in sweet Unity's Light.

The continents are thine cradles
    And every Race to Thee a child;
Each nursery, most gracefully girdles,
    The ocean blue, calm and mild.

Thy winds, waters and Thy soil,
    The same they are everywhere,
Nourishing all beings plebeian or royal
    Common for everyone to share.

Though actions and behaviours
    And conduct appear as diverse,
Yet one alone is the Power
    That animates this Universe.

Tho' many languages abound
    Greatly different in Peking or Rome,
One alone is the Primal Sound,
    The Root Vibration Om.

Tho' upon seeming external surface
    Man as diverse appears
This through Atomic Vision efface,
    Thus declare Sages and Seers.

All this is God only,
    There is no diversity.
This One Truth exists solely,
    Proclaims Man's eternal Unity.

In Unity we Live, by dissension fall
    The one Almighty is Father of all.
This Gracious Earth is the Mother of all
    Every human being is the brother of all.

As one Sun Illumines,
    The whole Earth outside
The Spirit Self-luminous,
    In Man doth reside.

Brightening and Lightening
    The chambers of his heart
Inspiring and indwelling
    Each Science, Religion and Art.

God is One, the Knowledge-Bliss,
    The same for all mankind,
Truth Supreme, One Reality is,
    Thus all true seekers do find.

The whole world to fasten
    As a golden cord spiritual
In sweet bonds of affection
    And true Brotherhood Eternal.

THE UNIVERSAL ANTHEM—II

(Thars: Sunaja, Sunaja, Sunaja Krishna)

Glory to Thee, O fair Mother Earth, common Parent of all,
The common sacred place of birth of all humanity.
All thy children, white or black, yellow, short or tall,
Bless one and all to know and feel this true Unity.

The continents are thine cradles and every race as child
Clothed with the blue and the oceans calm and mild.
Thy winds, water and soil, the same are everywhere
Nourishing every being, common for all to share.

Though conduct, actions and behaviour appear as diverse,
One alone is power that works in the Universe.
Though words and languages differ in Peking or in Rome
One alone the Primal Sound, the Root Vibration Om.

Though upon external surface Man as many appears
In Atman he is One, thus declare sages and seers.
All this is God alone, there is no diversity.
The only Truth of this Life is Man's essential Unity.

In Unity to live, but by dissension fall,
The one Almighty God is the Father of all.
This gracious Earth is the Mother of all.
Each Human being is the Brother of all.

As one Sun illumines the whole Earth outside,
The One Spirit Universal in Man doth reside
Brightening and Lightening the chambers of his heart;
Inspiring and indwelling each religion, Science and Art.

God is One, the Knowledge-Bliss, the same for all Mankind.
Truth Supreme, the One Reality, Spirit Transcendental
A golden cord spiritual, The whole world to bind,
In bonds of Love and Brotherhood and Unity Eternal.

CONTENTS

Chapter I
GOD, TRUTH OR BRAHMAN

1. Supreme Driver 33
2. Vishnumayam Jagat 33
3. One Essence 34
4. Truth 34
5. Cosmic Power House 35
6. Brahman Only Exists 36
7. Brahman Alone Is True 36
8. Brahman—The Seed 36
9. Everything Is in Essence Brahman 37
10. The Unseen Is Seen 37
11. Brahman and Maya 38
12. This World Is False 38

Chapter II
VAIRAGYA OR RENUNCIATION

1. Power of Renunciation 39
2. Yayati's Descent, Ascent 39
3. Life Here Is Transitory 40
4. Everything Is Transitory Here 41
5. Seek Not Mundane Life Any More 41
6. What Is This World? 41
7. Body Prison 42
8. Maya's Polish 43
9. Cut Meum and Tuum 43
10. Real Renunciation 44

Chapter III
WAKE UP, O MAN!

1. Wake Up, Friends!	45
2. Wake Up Now At Least	45
3. Weep Not, Stand Up!	46
4. Stand Up and Confess	47
5. What Is House?	47
6. What Is this Life of Mundane Power?	48
7. Who Is Really Happy?	48
8. Black Market	49
9. Be Straightforward	50
10. Passion By-products	50
11. Birds Are Very Happy	51
12. Various Sorts of Palm Oil!	52
13. Third World War	53
14. Atma Bahadurs	53
15. Mark My Word, O Golemole	54
16. Cure for Anxieties	55
17. Topics of the World	55
18. American Fashion	56
19. Refugees	57
20. I Am Pain: Thy Teacher	57
21. Do This One Big Business	60
22. Live in Boundary-less Realm	61
23. Be Courageous, Be Cheerful	61
24. Wake Up, Darling!	62

Chapter IV
GURU AND DISCIPLE

1. Supreme Guru	63

2. Siva the Supreme Guru 64
3. How Guru's Grace Works! 64
4. Three Kinds of Disciples 65
5. True Discipleship 65

Chapter V
INSTRUCTIONS ON SADHANA

1. Sadhana 66
2. Do Integral Sadhana 66
3. Song of Sadhana 67
4. To the Sadhaka 69
5. Man Wants Comfortable Samadhi 69
6. March On, Hero 70
7. March Forward, Fiery Soldier! 70
8. Serve and Be Dispassionate 71
9. For Whom Is the World Unreal? 71
10. Way To Beatitude 72
11. Good Life 72
12. Spiritual Appetisers 73
13. Way To Control The Senses 73
14. Story of Tongue 74
15. Hard It Is to Know 74
16. Kalpana 75
17. Watch the Kalpana 75
18. O Biscuit, It Is Luxury! 76
19. "Ahamta" and "Mamata" 76
20. Five Trunks in the Body 77
21. Method of Combination 78
22. Method of Conversion 78
23. Secret of Karma Yoga 79
24. O Wisdom, the Supreme Wealth! 79

25. All Wisdom Is Ever Within You 80
26. True Life 80
27. Tear Maya's Veil 80
28. Play on the Mind-Vina 81
29. Original Sin 81
30. Attain Perfection 82
31. Seek the Eternal 82
32. Liberation 83
33. The Abode of the Pure 83
34. Hear, Reflect and Meditate 84
35. Now, An Aptakama 84
36. As You Sow, So You Reap. 85
37. Listen, Friend! 85
38. Open the Eye of Your Heart. 86
39. Merging 86
40. The Day of Full Illumination 87
41. Three Obstacles 87
42. Whims of Sadhakas 88

Chapter VI
MIND AND ITS CONTROL

1. To The Mind 92
2. Listen; O Mind! 92
3. Soar High Like a Kite 93
4. Roam Not, O Mind! 93
5. Mind Is Very Treacherous. 93
6. Do Not Co-operate with the Mind 94

Chapter VII
PHILOSOPHY IN HUMOUR

1. Sunday Now Friday (Gandhi Day) 96

2. Do You Know this "I.C.S." and "P.C.S." 97
3. A Great F.F.S. and F.T.D. 97
4. Tamarind Brain. 98
5. Who Is "A-1 Loof" in Sirshasan 99
6. "Khoon Kharab Hogaya" 99
7. Solve this Riddle, Please! 100
8. The Greatest Miser 101
9. Freaks of Nature 101
10. Tirupati Shaving 102
11. "Uppuma-Coffee" Is Sweeter than Brahman! . 103
12. Story of an Applicant 104
13. Ode to Laddu. 105
14. U. N. O. 106

Chapter VIII
BHAKTI AND SELF-SURRENDER

1. Praise Be to the Lord 107
2. A Prayer 107
3. This Is My Prayer, O Lord! 108
4. Surrender and Be At Ease 108
5. Most Perfect Food. 109
6. The Inner Ruler. 109
7. Love—A Mighty Power 110
8. The Lord Runs a Mile 110
9. The Supreme Medicine 111
10. Name Is Nectar! 111
11. Drink this Celestial Ambrosia. 111
12. Panacea for Birth and Death 112
13. Drink Sivajnanamritam. 112
14. Philosophy of Stone Image 113

15. How Compassionate Is the Lord! 113
16. Glory to the Flute-bearer 114
17. Temple of My Heart. 114
18. My Vitthala Panduranga 115
19. Prabhu Mahima Stotra 115
20. Teach Me, O Lord! 115
21. Thou Art the Just Judge 116
22. Descend Now O Light. 116
23. O Hidden Joy. 117
24. My Crown 118
25. The Lord and His Sakti 118
26. Do Grant this Prayer, O Siva!. 119
27. The Abode of Silence 119
28. Siva's Grace 120
29. I Saw Him 120

Chapter IX
HEALTH, HYGIENE AND DIET

1. Body-Temple 121
2. Song of Vibhuti Yoga 121
3. Story of Vitamins 122
4. Health Menu 125
5. Fruits Hide the Atma 125

Chapter X
VEDANTIC MEDITATIONS

1. Who Am I? 127
2. How Free Am I! 128
3. I Am the All—I 129
4. I Am the All—II 129

5. I Am Nirmala Brahman 130
6. I Am Vijnana Ghana Brahman 130
7. I Am Svatantra Brahman 130
8. I Am Omkara Svaroopa 131
9. I Am Niravarana Brahma Svaroopa 131
10. I Am Parabrahma Svaroopa. 132
11. I Am Satya Svaroopa 132
12. I Am Chaitanya Svaroopa. 133
13. I Am Chinmatra Svaroopa 133
14. I Am Sukha Ghana Svaroopa. 133
15. I Am Ananda Ghana Svaroopa 134

Chapter XI
EXPERIENCES

1. Spiritual Experiences—I 135
2. Spiritual Experiences—II 136
3. I Drink the Nectar 136
4. Speechless Zone 137
5. That Exalted State 137
6. I Live in Silence! 138
7. Blissful Am I Now. 138
8. My Heart Is Brimful of Joy! 139
9. Welcome, Disease! Welcome!! 139
10. I Am Full Now 139
11. The Little 'I' Fused! 140
12. Samadhi 141
13. I Have Become That 141
14. I Found Him Out 142
15. Mysterious Experience 142
16. The Great Bhuma Experience. 143

Chapter XII
SANNYASIN, SAINT AND SAGE

1. Sannyasa... 144
2. Sannyasi... 144
3. Who Is a Sadhu?... 145
4. Who Is a Sage?... 146
5. Saint Narasi... 146
6. Vyavahara Jnani and Samadhi Jnani... 147

Chapter XIII
INDIA AND HER PEOPLE

1. Vande Mataram... 148
2. The Dawn of India's Freedom... 148
3. Glory to Great Men of India... 149
4. Glory To India's Great Women... 151
5. Hindus Wake Up... 151
6. Come Now, My Krishna!... 152

Chapter XIV
GARLAND OF YOGA

1. Man Is Like a Tree... 153
2. Head-strong Man... 153
3. Story of Horse "Edakku"... 154
4. Three "Pochus"... 155
5. Contagion... 155
6. This World—A Mysterious Show... 156
7. Strange Russia... 156
8. The Whole World Is Restless Now... 157
9. Evolution... 158
10. New Life in Destruction... 158

11. Sleep—Nature's Refresher 159
12. Ode to Sleep 159
13. Eka Sloki Gita 160

Chapter XV
SIVA AND HIS ABODE

1. Will of Siva 161
2. Siva the Source 161
3. Mine Is the Sovereignty Supreme 162
4. My Ministers 162
5. My Treasury Serves Me Well 163
6. My Sweet Abode 163
7. My Sadguru 164
8. Good Bye, O Death! 164
9. Goodbye 165
10. Siva's Magic 165
11. Tap the Source 166
12. Lord Viswanath 166
13. Invitation to Lord Dattatreya 167
14. Krishna, Join My Kirtan 167
15. The Divine Life Society, Rishikesh 168
16. Rules of the Sivananda Ashram 169

APPENDIX

1. Gandhiji's Death 171
2. Ode to Mahatma Gandhiji 171
3. Mira Behn 173

WAVES OF BLISS

Chapter I

GOD, TRUTH OR BRAHMAN

1. SUPREME DRIVER

THERE are pots, jugs etc.,
There must be a potter who has made all these.
There are chairs, benches and cots,
There must be a carpenter who has made all these.
There is the engine, there is the motor car,
There must be a driver for these.
There are vessels, firewood, rice etc.
There must be one who can cook food.

There must be an intelligent driver
To drive this body-engine,
That driver of this body-engine
Is the Supreme Driver of drivers,
He is the Lord or Brahman.

There are beings, trees, rivers and mountains,
There must be a creator for all these;
That creator is the Omnipotent Lord,
Who dwells in the chambers of your heart.
Know Him, the Supreme Driver and be happy for ever.

2. VISHNUMAYAM JAGAT

HARI is in earth, water, fire, air and ether.
Hari is in the sun, moon and stars.
Hari is in the mind, Prana and senses.
Hari is in flower, trees and vegetables.
Hari is in coffee, tea and cocoa.
Hari's face is turned everywhere.
He fills the whole universe.

He is the Indwelling Presence.
He dwells in the world, enveloping all over.
His Hands, Feet, Eyes and Heads are everywhere.
This entire world is His form only.
He is the earth, sun, fire and the Jiva.
All forms are Hari's forms only.
Therefore, hate not, injure not anybody.
Feel His Presence everywhere.
Behold Him in all forms.
Realise Him and be ever blissful.

3. ONE ESSENCE

I

BEHIND all names and forms is the One Nameless,
                              Formless Essence,
Behind all Governors is the One Supreme
                              Governor of Governors,
Behind all Lights is the one Light of lights,
Behind all sounds there is the soundless Supreme Silence,
Behind all teachers is the one Supreme Guru of Gurus,
Thou art That, Tat Tvam Asi, O Ram!

II

Behind all these perishable is the
                              One Imperishable Absolute,
Behind all these motions is the one motionless Infinite,
Behind time, minutes and days is the one timeless
                              Eternity,
Behind hatred, riots and wars, is the one hidden Love,—
Thou art That, Tat Tvam Asi, O Ram!

4. TRUTH

TRUTH is within yourself. It endures for ever.
It exists in the past, present and future.
There is an innermost centre within yourself,

Where Truth abides in fullness.
Truth is Existence, Knowledge and Bliss Absolute.
Truth is the Absolute, the Infinite, the Eternal.
Truth is Satyam, Jnanam, Anantam.
Truth is Self-luminous, Self-existent, Self-contained.
Truth is Atman, Brahman, Purusha.
Truth is your centre, ideal and goal.
Live in Truth; meditate on Truth;
Realise Truth by speaking Truth,
And by leading a Truthful life!

5. COSMIC POWER HOUSE

THE individual souls are like the electric bulbs,
The bulbs get their light from the power house;
The Jivas get their power from Brahman,
The Infinite Cosmic Power House.

The bulb imagines "I am independent."
It vainly boasts of its effulgence and power.
It has no idea of its source.
When the current fails,
It puts its head in shame,
It repents and weeps.

Even so, the Jiva brags out of his egoism,
"I know everything, I can do anything."
"That is my bungalow, she is my wife,
There is no God."

He has no idea of Brahman, the source.
He eats, drinks, dresses and sleeps,
He leads a miserable Asuric life,
He repents and weeps in old age.
O fool! O dunce! Know the source,
Through purity, devotion, Tapas and meditation,
And enjoy supreme peace and eternal bliss.

6. BRAHMAN ONLY EXISTS

THERE is neither Maya nor Maya's activity.
There is neither Moha nor tempting world.
There is neither egoism nor Chitta.
There is neither body nor doer nor Karma.
There is neither instrument nor sight.
There is neither seer nor knower.
There is neither Upadhi nor Avidya.
There is no Sadhana Sampatti.
There is neither Sravana nor Manana.
There is neither Samadhi nor Sadhana.
There is neither bondage nor liberation.
There is only the self-existent Brahman!

7. BRAHMAN ALONE IS TRUE

THAT which is seen is utter falsehood;
That which is heard is also falsehood;
That which is smelt is entire lie;
That which is tasted is all lie;
That which is touched is pure falsehood;
That which is enjoyed is all falsehood;
That which is thought of is a terrible lie;
That Eternal, Pure, Self-luminous Brahman
Which is Colourless, Tasteless and Formless—
That alone is true;
That is the only Living Reality;
That is the only Living Truth;
That is the only Living Presence;
Realise this and be free for ever.

8. BRAHMAN—THE SEED

SEED is one:
But the fruits, flowers, leaves are countless;
It produces countless seeds.
A very big tree comes out of a single seed:

Even so Brahman, the Seed of this world is One,
But the creatures are countless and diverse.
The Tree bespeaks of the Glory of the Lord;
This world proclaims the Omnipotence of the Lord.
Every object is the Vibhuti of the Lord.
Feel the Presence of the Lord everywhere
Think deeply and become Silent.

9. EVERYTHING IS IN ESSENCE BRAHMAN

THIS world is in essence Brahman only.
All objects are in essence Brahman only.
Everything is really Chinmatra Brahman.
Everything is really Chinmaya Brahman.
Akasa, air, fire are really Anandamaya Brahman.
Water and earth are really Chinmatra Brahman.
Jnana, Jneya, Drishya, Drik are really
                              Anandamaya Brahman.
Individual souls are in essence Satchidananda Brahman.
Substratum for this world is Ananda Svaroopa Brahman.
The essence of all objects is Ananda Brahman.
Mind is really Anandamaya Brahman.
The senses are really Chinmaya Brahman.

10. THE UNSEEN IS SEEN

THE Petromax does not talk,
But it shines and sheds light all around;
The Jessamine does not speak,
But it wafts its fragrance everywhere;
The Lighthouse sounds no drum,
But sends its friendly light to the mariner;—
The Unseen beats no gong,
But its omnipresence is felt
By the dispassionate and the discriminating sage.

11. BRAHMAN AND MAYA

THIS world is unreal, yet it appears.
It is an effect of illusory Maya.
Though it appears, it is unreal.
Maya and Brahman cannot co-exist,
Just as cat and rat cannot remain in a cage;
One should go away;
Cat and rat are opposites.
If you behold Maya, you cannot see Brahman.
If you realise Brahman, Maya vanishes.
If you see snake, there is no rope;
If you see the rope, the snake disappears.
Maya and Brahman possess opposite qualities.
Brahman is Sat-Chit-Ananda,
Existence-Knowledge-Bliss;
Maya is Asat, Jada, Duhkha, unreal, insentient
             and painful.
If there is a rubber (false) cat, real rat can remain
             and vice versa.

12. THIS WORLD IS FALSE

THE elements are false.
This world is false.
Creation, preservation, destruction are false.
Enjoyment is false, bondage is false.
All objects are false, destiny is false.
Wealth, house, pleasure, pain are false.
Mind and speech are false.
Celestial gods are false.
Meditation is false.
That which is thought of by the mind is false.
Touch, hearing, seeing, smelling, tasting are false.
I, you, he, this, that are false.
Time is false.
All appearances are false.
Brahman or the Absolute alone is real.

Chapter II

VAIRAGYA OR RENUNCIATION

1. POWER OF RENUNCIATION

YUDHISHTHIRA passed by the side of Naraka (hell)
Because he uttered once a harmless lie.
The dwellers of Naraka rejoiced very much.
Their pangs were alleviated
Because they had Yudhishthira by their side.
The Viman came to take Yudhishthira to heaven.
Yudhishthira declined to enter the Viman.
He said: "Thousands rejoice by my presence here.
I will give all my merits;
Let these dwellers of hell go to heaven;
I do not mind remaining here."

Countless Vimans came to take these people.
Then a great Viman came to take Yudhishthira also.
Yudhishthira said: "I cannot come;
I have given all my merits to them."
The Messengers said:
"You have increased your merits millionfold
Through your renunciation.
Come to heaven now, here is the Viman."
Yudhishthira also went to heaven.
Such is the power of renunciation;
Therefore practise renunciation.

2. YAYATI'S DESCENT, ASCENT

KING Yayati was proud of his Tapas:
He belittled the Tapas of Rishis;
The Rishis cursed Yayati,

"You will soon fall from heaven!"
Yayati entreated the Rishis
"Let me fall in a place
Where Tapaswins dwell."
Rishis said, "Tatasthu, be it so."
Yayati went to heaven
But he soon had a fall:
He was coming down;
His great grand-children
Who were doing severe Tapas
Noticed his downfall.
They said to Yayati,
"Take our Tapas and go back to heaven."
Yayati replied,
"I am a Kshatriya, I do not beg;
Keep your Tapas with you."
The power of this renunciation
Made him again ascend to heaven;
Such is the power of renunciation,
Therefore practise renunciation.

3. LIFE HERE IS TRANSITORY

LIFE is like the lightning flash.
It is fleeting and transitory.
It fades quickly like the rainbow,
Like the impression on the water.
It is like a bubble or dream,
Shadow, mist or mirage.
And yet man thinks that life is permanent here.
This is Maya's delusion, mind's jugglery.
It is deception of the senses.
Wake up, O Man! from this long slumber.
Understand Maya's tricks and learn to discriminate.
Attain knowledge of the Infinite
And enjoy Immortal Bliss of Brahman.

VAIRAGYA OR RENUNCIATION

4. EVERYTHING IS TRANSITORY HERE

FOR a moment saw I the wealth of a rich man,
For a moment saw I the Rulership of a King,
For a moment saw I the power of a Dictator and a Premier,
For a moment saw I the strength of an athlete,
For a moment saw I the beauty of a damsel,
For a moment saw I the position of an Officer,
For a moment saw I the love of husband and wife,
For a moment saw I the intelligence of Professors,
For a moment saw I the friendship of comrades,
For a moment saw I the pleasures of people here!
"O Man! Seek the Eternal, and be ever blissful!"

5. SEEK NOT MUNDANE LIFE ANY MORE

HAVE you not understood the nature of mundane life?
Have you not realised the magnitude of human sufferings?
Have you not seen sorrow, pain and ill in all things here?
Have you been really benefited by the earthly life?
Have your wife and children given you real happiness?
Have money, power, name and fame, car, bungalows,
Given you real lasting solace?
Have you got a single, sincere friend here?
Have you really grasped the nature of Maya and Samsara?
Come thou not back again to birth here!
Abandon ruthlessly this clinging to this earthly life!
The "will to live and enjoy here".
Happiness here in objects is a will-o-the-wisp,
The *ignis fatuus*, an illusory mirage;
Serve, love, purify, meditate on the Immortal Atman.
You will soon attain Supreme Blessedness.

6. WHAT IS THIS WORLD?

BRAHMAN appears as this world.
This is an effect of Maya.

It is Virat Svaroopa.
There are two, three and five here.
The two are the pairs of opposites.
Virtue and vice, good and bad, right and wrong.
There is a play of three Gunas.
Sattva opposes Rajas and Tamas.
The five elements constitute this world.
This world binds a passionate man.
There is no world for a liberated sage.
It is the mind that projects this world;
Manomatra Jagat, Manah Kalpita Jagat.
There is no world in deep sleep.
Transcend this world of two, three and five
Through dispassion, discrimination and meditation;
And rest peacefully in the ever blissful Atman.

7. BODY PRISON

THE body is the prison house;
This is the greatest jail.
The senses are the guards.
This world is the fixed place of suffering.
Through Karmas you have entered this jail,
To reap the fruits of your actions.
O man! Come out of this prison-house quickly,
By identifying with the all-pervading Brahman,
By abandoning "mine-ness," and "I-ness",
By annihilating cravings, and desires,
By giving up likes and dislikes,
By meditating on the Supreme Self,
By constant thinking "I am Brahman."

8. MAYA'S POLISH

MAYA is the greatest artist.
She is the greatest juggler also.
Her tricks worldlings can hardly detect.
She deludes the passionate and the uncautious.

VAIRAGYA OR RENUNCIATION

She hides the real and makes the unreal appear.
She is the illusory power of the Lord.
She projects this world for His Lila.
She causes false glittering,
And entraps the deluded Jivas.
She does a little electroplating work;
She gives a little polish and softness to the skin;
Man is entrapped in the snare of a woman.
He forgets that behind the skin is raw flesh,
Mucous, pus, phlegm and excreta.
He is attracted by colours, sounds,
Soft touch, taste and sweet-meats.
He indulges, gets all sorts of diseases.
He is caught in the wheel of birth and death.
Honour, name, fame, titles are her tempting bait.
O Man! O Fool! Wake up from the slumber of ignorance!
Develop dispassion, discrimination and enquire
                              "Who am I".
You will free yourself from Maya's clutches.
You will attain the Eternal Bliss of Brahman!

9. CUT MEUM AND TUUM

CUT and tear this veil of Meum (Mine) and Tuum (Thine).
Destroy all sorts of mundane relationship:
Kaaka, Chacha, Bathija,
Mamma, Ammanji, Babee, Beebee.
Keep relationship with the Absolute alone!
This world is empty, hollow and essenceless;
The charm of youth is fleeting;
Money passes from one hand to another;
Millionaire becomes beggar;
Young damsel becomes an old woman.
Build not bungalows here;
You will be attached to them;
You will forget the real Home.
Be ever unattached and free!

10. REAL RENUNCIATION

ABANDONING all actions is no renunciation.
Living in Himalayan cave is no renunciation.
Eating fruits and milk only is no renunciation.
To be nude is no renunciation.
Wearing orange robe is no renunciation.
Shaving the head is no renunciation.
Leaving the world is no renunciation.
Renunciation of egoism and mine-ness is real renunciation.
Renunciation of cravings and Vasanas is real renunciation.
Renunciation of all attachment is real renunciation.
Freedom from Kartritwa-bhoktritwa Bhavana is real renunciation.
Freedom from Bheda-buddhi is real renunciation.
Abandonment of Dehadhyasa is real renunciation.
Living in Atman is real renunciation.
Brahmanishtha is real renunciation.
Freedom from Prakriti and Tattvas is real renunciation.

Chapter III

WAKE UP, O MAN!

1. WAKE UP, FRIENDS!

THE wealth of this world,
The knowledge of this objective universe,
Friends, relatives, wife and children,
Bungalows, motor cars and cities,
Gardens, parks and hill stations,
Food, drinks, coffee, uppuma,
Iddalis, sambar, lemon squash,
Hotels, restaurants and clubs,
Position, titles, diplomas and colleges,
Are all jugglery of Maya.
They are false, illusory and deceptive.
They are shadow, bubble and dream.
Wake up, friends! at once;
Realise the Inner Reality,
And be happy for ever!

2. WAKE UP NOW AT LEAST

O MAN! You are living in vain.
You have wasted your life.
You have not cut off your desires.
You have not severed the ties or bonds.
You have not worshipped Lord Hari.
You have not chanted the eight letters.
Fie on thee! O miserable wretch!
Wake up now at least.
There is still hope for you.
Lord Hari is most gracious.

Sing His Glory. Do Kirtan. Repeat His Name.
Serve Saints. Speak of Badri,
Tirupati, Pandharpur, Puri, Mathura,
Brindavan, Ayodhya, Bhadrachal,
Dwaraka, Srirangam, Guruvayur;
You will soon attain immortal Bliss.

3. WEEP NOT, STAND UP!

GIVE up this Moha or delusion.
The soul dies not, decays not.
It is immortal, unchanging, eternal.
You do not gain anything by shedding tears.
"My son, My darling, My husband: you are dead!"
By lamenting you make the soul earth-bound,
And hinder his march towards heaven.
Death is for regeneration and growth.
Do not be afraid of death.
Say "Welcome death! Welcome."
It is like changing of old clothes.
In reality there is neither birth nor death.
Birth and death are illusory scenes,
In the Mayaic drama of mundane life.
It is shadow, dream, mirage, bubble, snake in the rope.
Grieve not; regret not; fear not.
Be bold, be cheerful, be courageous, be adamant.
He still lives in your heart.
His actions and qualities serve as beacon-light,
To guide you to lead the Life Divine.
He is still guiding you
From his new abode of perennial joy and eternal
                                                             sunshine.
Substance or Brahman alone exists.
"Thou art That" "Tat Tvam Asi" in essence.
Yield not to impotence, O Ram! O Sushila!
Shake off this paltry chicken-heartedness.
Stand up like a lion and roar OM OM OM.

4. STAND UP AND CONFESS

O MAN! How ignorant thou art!
Just as the owl likes darkness;
So you like doing wicked deeds.
You take pleasure in doing sins.
You know by experience the pain
That comes from falsehood and lust;
And the happiness from truth and purity.
And yet you have lost your understanding;
You continue doing evil actions.
What a shame! What a deplorable state!
Stand up with a contrite heart.
Confess, pray fervently before the Lord.
Seek the company of saints and sages.
You, too, will soon attain salvation.

5. WHAT IS HOUSE?

IT is the pleasure centre of ignorant Jivas.
It is the place where "Bhabi" and "Beebi" fight,
Where mother-in-law quarrels with the daughter-in-law.
One child is sick and cries for "laddus".
Another is passing motions in a corner.
The eldest son is suffering from typhoid.
The second daughter has just become a widow.
The second son lost his job
And is in the role of unemployment.
He is troubling his father for money
To open a small shop.
The father was worried and left his house
To take Sannyasa in Rishikesh.
The third son went in search of his father.
He showed his father's photo to the Swami.
The Swami replied "Search in Uttarkasi".
The old mother is weeping in the house.
Such is the pleasure-centre of Jivas;

And yet man passionately clings to the house
On account of Maya Moha.
O Man! Become "aniketha";
And dwell for ever in the abode of Immortal Bliss,
Thy original house of pristine purity!

6. WHAT IS THIS LIFE OF MUNDANE POWER?

THE mind is ever restless.
It is ever suspicious.
One cannot move freely in the streets.
He is in need of a body guard and military force.
He is in need of pilot cars.
He is always thinking:
"Someone may throw bomb; some one may shoot;
Someone may stab me."
He is looking here and there.
He cannot enjoy good sleep.

O Man! Look at the Jivanmukta.
He is ever carefree, happy and joyful.
King Yadu admired Sage Dattatreya
And fell at his feet for instructions.
Emperor Alexander was struck with amazement,
When he saw a blessed Sage
Ever sitting peacefully on a block of stone.
King Janaka bowed his head at the feet of
                                    Sage Yajnavalkya.
Strive not for earthly power and possession.
It is all illusory and painful.
Cultivate dispassion and discrimination.
Renounce, introspect, meditate,
And live peacefully in the Immortal Soul.
All Riddhis and Siddhis will roll under your feet.

7. WHO IS REALLY HAPPY

HE who has studied scriptures and Puranas;
He who possesses immense wealth;

He who wields all sorts of Magisterial powers;
He who holds the highest status or position;
He who moves in cars and aeroplanes;
He who takes lunches in Taj Mahal Hotel;
He who is a Dictator or President of States;
He who is an Emperor, Premier or Governor General;
He who lives in bungalows in Hill Stations;
He who lives with young damsels;
He who has developed various powers or Siddhis;
He who is a M.A. Ph.D., or D.Sc., or D.Litt.;
He is not happy.

He alone is happy
Who has controlled his mind and the senses;
Who is free from egoism, lust and pride;
Who has destroyed all cravings and desires;
Who is humble, simple, truthful and merciful;
Who is immersed in the bliss of Brahman.

8. BLACK MARKET

WHEREVER there is Tamas or darkness,
There is black market;
Wherever there is ignorance or Avidya,
There is black market;
Wherever there is untruthful transaction,
There is black market.
The wife or husband becomes unfaithful,
The disciple speaks ill of his Guru,
The superior gets bribes from the subordinates,
Here is black market.

Wherever there is greed and selfishness,
There is black market.
The Jnana Surya does not shine here,
Unity and cosmic love run away from here,
Satyam, Subham do not abide here,
Peace does not reign here.

Black market dealer has no Tejas:
He is a slayer of Atman,
His face is coal-tarred,
He is a burden on this earth;
His ill-earned wealth will soon vanish,
For he has cut the throats of his brothers;—
He will directly proceed to the darkest hells.

Therefore, O Man! Abandon black-marketing.
Be truthful and attain eternal bliss.

9. BE STRAIGHTFORWARD

FILL not your pockets by plundering the poor.
The walls of palaces of big Zamindars
Are built out of the blood of the poor tenants.
They will suffer severely in the hell
For their deeds of cruelty.
They will be born in the wombs of animals.
So also those who have become rich
By charging heavy interest, black-marketing
And other crooked ways in business.

Be straight and simple in your speech.
Twist not your speech and its meaning,
By intelligent methods and diplomatic turns.
Abandon text-torturing in religious discussions,
Twisting and confounding Penal Code
To have a roaring practice at the Bar.
Be truthful, God fearing and compassionate.
The doors of Immortal Bliss will be open unto thee.

10. PASSION BY-PRODUCTS

CHILDREN are the passion by-products
Of Mummy and Daddy,
Mamma and Pappa,
Amma and Appa.
The lust fire melts the butter mind;

The products are multiplying with great speed
As there is no self-restraint.
Man does not think at that moment
Whether he will be able to support them or not.
Beggars are multiplying rapidly.
It is a heinous crime
To bring forth a child
If you cannot support and educate him.
Study "Practice of Brahmacharya" and practise.

Children are sources of misery.
They bind you to the wheel of Samsara.
They intensify Moha and attachment.
They are Maya's tempting baits.
Lead a life of single-blessedness,
And reach the goal quickly.

11. BIRDS ARE VERY HAPPY

THE birds and animals are very happy.
They are free from cares, worries and anxieties.
They possess more self-restraint.
Thy are not greedy, lustful and proud.
They do not care for possessions.
They are not dissatisfied and discontented.
They do not weep for their sins.
They do not loot, stab and burn houses.
They do not fly to U.N.O.
To represent their grievances.
They do not go to Vienna
For any operation or consultation.
They do not build bungalows.
They do not want "Penicillin" or "M. & B."
They eat some herbs here and there
And maintain wonderful health.
They do not want sweater and over-coat.
Not one kneels to another;
Not one is unhappy over the entire universe.

O Foolish Man! Learn lessons from them,
And roam about happily for ever!

12. VARIOUS SORTS OF PALM OIL!

SOME get Christmas presents;
Some get their share of mangoes,
Clothes, dhall, rice, etc.;
Some get 5%, 10%;
Some get half and half, fifty-fifty;
Sometimes the mem-sab gets a cheque
And some sovereigns at the backdoor;
For some a big envelope is placed in their pockets;
Some get a gift of a motor car;
This is another form of decent tip or palm oil.
Intelligent people adopt intelligent methods;
Greater the culture, greater the trick;
Greater the intelligence, more refined is the method;
Then the work is done at once.
Then the signature and sanction come immediately.
All these people kill their conscience and soul.
This will continue from birth to birth.
They do not know what they are doing.
What a great delusion!
They get a direct passport to Raurava hell.
Many have become rich through palm oil.
But the money will go to the doctors,
Thieves and dacoits.
Sons will squander the money.
The hands will be affected with leprosy.
O Ignorant Man! Give up this corruption.
Live within your means.
Lead a virtuous life.
Vedanayagam put his wife in jail,
For accepting some betel leaves.
What a noble, exalted soul!
Be pure like him.
Slay not thy soul and conscience.

Spiritual wealth is the inexhaustible wealth.
Be pure and reach the goal in this very birth.

13. THIRD WORLD WAR

THE third world war is threatening.
It will quell the pride of the nations.
Where is Japan now? Where is Germany now?
Where is Hitler now? Where is Mussolini now?
Both parties are now counting their atom bombs.
Atom bombs are their asset and strength.
Everybody wants to be a leader.
Everybody wants to rule over others.
Everybody wants power.
Everybody wants to be a President or Dictator.
Everybody wants to rule over the whole world.
Nobody wants to tap the source by looking within.

Ignorance is the cause of war.
Passion and greed excite the man,
And make him forget his divine nature,
Universal brotherhood, oneness of humanity,
The teachings of Prophets, the truth of Scriptures.
He develops headstrong and weak-hearted nature.
He hates and kills others ruthlessly.
How overwhelming is delusion!
It hurls down even mighty intelligent persons,
Into the dark abyss of ignorance.
O Man! Wake up from the slumber of ignorance;
Know thyself and be free.
Understand the oneness of life and consciousness;
Learn to discriminate and become wise.

14. ATMA BAHADURS

OLD Rao Bahadurs feel miserable now;
Because they have lost their titles.
But old memories bring them elation;
Just as the bankrupt gets some pleasure

When he goes through old account books,
So also they get some pleasure
When they look at their letter-heads,
And think of their past tea parties,
When people call them even now "Rao Bahadur Saheb."
Poor Rao Bahadurs! Open your eyes!
Do not be carried away by false titles.
Once you were totally blind and so you were duped;
Become a real Bahadur of Bahadurs now
By disciplining the mind and subjugating the senses,
And resting in your own Satchidananda Svaroop.
Glory to such "Atma Bahadurs"!
Indian Union wants such Atma Bahadurs now.
May the world abound with Atma Bahadurs!

15. MARK MY WORD, O GOLEMOLE

A WOMAN who knits is attached to knitting;
Moves about with the needles and thread.
A son of a great Pundit who is attached to smoking
Goes to take water in the Ganga with a cigarette.
He who is very fond of newspaper reading
Always keeps newspaper in his hands;
He dies if he does not get newspaper in a day;
He runs to the post office or his neighbour.
He who is fond of gambling, drinking or horse race,
Dies without it even for a day.
He who goes to cinema, plays cards,
Feels as a fish out of water without them.
O foolish man! Give even a bit of your mind
To the Lord, His Kirtan and Japa.
You will float in the ocean of bliss.
Mark my word! O Golemole!
Become wise and turn a new chapter
In the book of your life!

16. CURE FOR ANXIETIES

YOU have anxiety for food.
When the stomach is full,
You have anxiety for cloth and money.
When you have money,
You have anxiety for the body.
When cough and fever trouble you,
You are anxious "Will this be T. B. or Pneumonia?"
Even when you are healthy,
You are anxious about your wife and children.
"My fifth daughter is pregnant;
My fourth son has appeared for M.B.B.S. Examination."
Even when everything is all right,
You are anxious about your business.
Even when business is flourishing,
You are anxious "That man will stab me;
This man will loot me, and throw bomb;
I may die of cholera or typhoid."
O Ignorant man! Turn your mind towards God.
Repeat His Name, sing His glory, meditate.
All anxieties will come to an end.
You will enjoy eternal bliss!

17. TOPICS OF THE WORLD

OH! What a Great joy!
    Hon'ble Sir Khedkar is blessed with a son;
Maharaja Ram Singh has married Svarnalatha;
    Hon'ble Andakar is now the Premier.

Oh! What a great Sorrow
    Mr. Robertson has divorced Elizabeth;
Bhushan Kumari was kidnapped;
    Raj Kumar's only son died yesterday;

O! What a terrible scene!
    One hundred houses were burnt last night,

Three hundred persons were stabbed,
  Fifty bombs were thrown on the Station.
There was earthquake at Lucknow,
  There was cyclone at Amsterdam.

Milk is very, very dear at Badri,
  Apple is very, very cheap at Srinagar.
Sambhar is nice, Rasagulla is fine.
  Sweet pudding is lovely, Golguppa is appetizing.

O Man! Give up these little talks,
  Talk on Brahman, the Eternal Bliss.
Soar high and attain the Infinite,
  Through purity and meditation.

18. AMERICAN FASHION

FASHION is raging in America.
A woman always carries her powder bag,
  compact and manicure.
Even in the street she looks at her face in the mirror,
Applies rouge, lipstick, powder, pencils the brow.
Even at the dining table she does the same.
She has no sense of modesty.
Even in dream she applies powder and rouge.
This artificial painting mars her natural beauty;
She appears like a doll or a devil.
It takes three hours to dress her hair
And apply cutex to the nails.
She is ever thinking of her body alone.
She worships the flesh, bone and hair,
The leather bag of pus and wool.
What a great shame and folly!
She is a slayer of Atma or the pure soul.
Such women are horizontal beings without tail.
This infection has spread to India also.
Indian women also imitate—
The monkey mind ever imitates.
O women! Abandon this devilish fashion.

WAKE UP, O MAN!

Physical beauty is skin deep and fading.
Become pure; simple and natural.
Slay not your inner soul.
Think ceaselessly of the blissful Atma.
"The Beauty of beauties", Infinite Beauty;
And attain freedom, perfection and immortality.

19. REFUGEES

PUNJABIS are in trouble.
They have lost their relations and houses,
Their property, and valuable belongings.
Bombay is full of refugees.
Some are lying on the roadside.
Some have neither clothing nor blankets.
Chill penury is afflicting.
Stomach is severely pinching,
And yet "Ram Nam" does not come out of their mouth!
Their minds are not turned towards God.
They have not understood the unreality of this world.
How powerful is Maya!
How infatuating is delusion, Moha!
How potent is Avidya or ignorance!
How strong is attachment!
O Lord! Grant them peace, devotion and wisdom;
Tear their veil of ignorance.

20. I AM PAIN: THY TEACHER

I

O MAN! You curse me, blame me,
You hate me and frown at me,
You think, I am cruel and heartless;
You try to slay me with anaesthetics,
With Chloroform and Bromides;
You attack me with anodynes,
Sedatives and opiates;
You phone to the doctors

And run to the hospitals,
You fly to Vienna and hill stations,
You wire to your friends and relations;
You approach the saints of Himalayas
For Buties or herbs;
You do Mrityunjaya Japa and Havan,
You burn incense and pray—
To kill the Teacher
Who warns you,
Who comes to help and bless you!

II

I am not your enemy—
I am your sincere friend!
I am a messenger from God,
I am an angel from heaven,—
To teach you wisdom,
To instil in your heart
Mercy and dispassion,
To turn your mind towards God,
To destroy your intense clinging
To things mundane—
That are perishable and illusory.
I am your guide and silent Teacher!
I am pain, the best thing in this world,
I am an eye-opener, soul-awakener,
I am an inspirer and thriller;
I come to remind you of God,
To point to you the Divine Path,
To make you desist from evil ways,
To make you practise virtues, good habits.
You have really misunderstood me.

I am a mental Vritti in the mind-lake,
I am only absence of pleasure,
I co-exist with pleasure—
I am the other side of the coin of pleasure-pain.

WAKE UP, O MAN!

I am the cause of the starting of philosophy,
I am the cause for man's Purushartha—
I am the cause for man's aspiration:
I set the mind of philosophers to think,
I make the Yogis to start Sadhana,
I make the sages to practise meditation,
I make a worldly man a Superman.

III

You failed to observe the laws of health—
The rules of hygiene and right-living;
You took Rajasic and Tamasic foods,
You were not regular in doing exercise,
You did not practise Pranayama and Asanas,
You did not pray and meditate;
You were immoderate in your food—
You did not take a balanced diet,
You did not bask in the sun,
You slept in ill-ventilated rooms,
You took too much of sweetmeats,
You drank impure water,
You hated and injured your neighbours,
You were lustful, malicious and greedy,
You took meat, fish and eggs
And developed gout, rheumatism and albuminaria;
You married a third wife,
You were a heavy smoker in the club,
You drank liquors in the hotels;
You took bribes and cheated in business;
You twisted the truth in the courts,
And by clever advocacy
Sent innocent men
To the prison and the gallows;
You injected water into the veins
And charged heavily for injections;—
And so, I come to you
To heal, teach and guide!

IV

Understand now at least
My secret and good nature,
My interest in your well-being.
Lead a virtuous life,
Practise simple living and high thinking,
Lead a natural life,
Observe the laws of health and hygiene—
Eat simple food, a well-balanced diet,
Take only vegetarian diet;
Practise Ahimsa, Satyam, Brahmacharya,
Lead the Life Divine,
Remain as a Brahmacharin,
Or better still, take to Sannyasa
After equipping yourself with 'four';
Practise Sadhana in Ananda Kutir,
Attend the Sadhana Weeks,
And the Training Courses,
Go through the "Divine Life" magazine,
Study "Spiritual Lessons" "Aphorisms",
"The Necessity for Sannyasa"
And practice the precepts contained therein;
Remember Lord Viswanath always,
Take bath in the Ganga and purify.
Then I will depart and leave you,
I will not trouble you any longer.
Love me, believe me, heed my message
I will give you peace, bliss, immortality,
I will surely bless you:
This is my definite promise, friend!
Goodbye, comrade! Be cheerful!

21. DO THIS ONE BIG BUSINESS

BUSINESS makes a man very rich quickly.
He rolls in wealth and Rolls Royce.
It makes him a bankrupt and beggar also in no time.

It is full of worries, anxieties,
Lies, black-marketism and cut-throatism.
It makes him forget God.
It takes him straight-away to hell.
It does not give him real, lasting happiness.

Hence do this one big business alone.
Have transactions with the one Supreme Lord,
The source of all wealth, power and bliss.
Put all the money in Siva's Unlimited Bank.
Earn the inexhaustible spiritual wealth of the Infinite,
Through Japa, Kirtan, meditation and enquiry.
Sing Sivoham, Sivoham, Sivoham, Soham;
Sat-chit-ananda Svaroopoham!

22. LIVE IN BOUNDARY-LESS REALM

HOW did this boundary question come
In that boundary-less Infinite?
Boundary arises out of ignorance.
It splits and causes dissentions.
It limits, constricts and circumscribes.
It narrows the vision and contracts the heart.
There is really neither Kalsastan; nor Pathanstan;
Neither England-sthan; nor American-sthan.
Neither Russian Zone, nor U.S. Zone.
O ignorant little man! Give up fighting.
Live in the eternal, boundary-less realm
Of perennial joy and immortal Bliss!

23. BE COURAGEOUS, BE CHEERFUL

O MAN! Be courageous; be cheerful.
Do not fret and fume for little things.
Be serene; keep poise; be joyful.
Abandon all cares, worries and anxieties.
Smile, laugh, dance in ecstasy.
Why do you look so sad and cheerless?
Wipe away all the intricacies and complexities of life;

Abandon sorrow, grief, delusion and infatuation.
Thy abode is the immaculate Brahmic seat of
                                    Eternal Bliss;
Thou art ever perfect, free and independent.
Thou art not born.
Thou art immortal, decayless and changeless.
Thou art Lord of lords, Sun of suns;
Thou art Emperor of emperors; King of kings.

24. WAKE UP, DARLING!

WAKE UP, darling, wake up!
Forget not your essential, divine nature.
"I am a Brahmin", "I am a doctor",
"She is my wife", "This is my house",
"He is my daddy", "She is my mummy",
"He is my son", "I did this", "I enjoyed that",
"I am the body", "I am tall and black"—
This is a terrible falsehood.
Thou art neither the body, nor the mind,
Abandon "I-ness" and "mine-ness",
Agency, doership and enjoyership.
Thou art the "Absolute", "Thou art Atman"—
"Tat Tvam Asi", "Tat Tvam Asi"—
"Thou art That", "That thou art"!

Chapter IV

GURU AND DISCIPLE

1. SUPREME GURU

THE Lord that liveth in the chambers of the heart;
The Lord that removeth the veil of ignorance;
The Lord that showerest grace;
The Lord that inspireth devotion;
The Lord that revealeth the Truth;
The Lord that governeth this universe;
The Lord that lieth behind the names and forms;
He is my Supreme Guru.
My adorations and prostrations to this Supreme Guru!

2. SIVA THE SUPREME GURU

(Dakshinamurthy)

ENTHRONED on His seat on Himalaya's or
Trans-Himalaya's heights,
Siva taking youth's form human, exquisite, everlasting,
Teaches reverend sages sitting at His feet
Lessons of Eternal Wisdom, vanquishing
Doubt, darkness, death, despair and delusion.

He, the Teacher of teachers—the Supreme Teacher—
His method unique. His teachings flash from heart
                                              to heart,
Soul to soul, which no spoken words convey,
His silence nevertheless their doubts destroys.
This is the wonder of wonders!

His hand is raised in benediction over this ancient land,
On which He casts His south-ward gaze,

Just as He "Conscious many faced" blesses
                              all races and climes
Facing them as they spread in front.
Eternal Watcher! Standing sentinel, shedding Love
For earth's constant welfare.
For as He seeth and silently rules,
Naught can go wrong in His world,
In whom all beings sentient or inert abide,
Whose one will ordains that good overcometh evil
And righteousness ever prevails even if seemingly
                                              delayed.
All teachers of whatever degree represent
Him in all good things they impart,
And His power goeth to bless both the
                              teacher and the taught.

3. HOW GURU'S GRACE WORKS!

IF an aspirant sticks to the path tenaciously,
This is the grace of the Guru.
If he resists when temptation assails him,
This is the grace of the Guru.
If people receive him with love and reverence,
This is the grace of the Guru.
If he gets all bodily wants,
This is the grace of the Guru.
If he gets encouragement and strength,
When he is in despair and despondency,
This is the grace of the Guru.
If he gets over the body-consciousness
And rests in his own Ananda Svaroopa,
This is the grace of the Guru.
Feel his grace at every step,
And be sincere and truthful to him.

4. THREE KINDS OF DISCIPLES

THEY are "Pooth", "Supooth" and "Kapooth".
"Pooth" is one
Who takes care of the Guru's Ashram;
And nicely continues his activities.

"Supooth" is one
Who develops beautifully the Ashram,
Expands his work
And brings more fame to his Guru.

"Kapooth" is one
Who lives on what the Guru has earned
Closes the Ashram quickly;
And brings bad name to his Guru.

Vivekananda, Sraddhananda, Annie Besant
Were all "Supooth" disciples.
Friends! Never become a "Kapooth";
Try to become at least a "Pooth"!

5. TRUE DISCIPLESHIP

TRUE discipleship opens the vision:
It kindles the spiritual fire;
It awakens the dormant faculties.
It is most necessary in one's journey
Along the spiritual path.
Guru and disciple become one.
Guru blesses, guides and inspires the disciple;
He transmits, transforms, spiritualises him.
Glory to Sadguru and true disciple.

Chapter V

INSTRUCTIONS ON SADHANA

1. SADHANA

IF YOU give up reading newspapers,
If you abandon playing cards,
If you reduce your sleep,
If you reduce your time spent
In playing tennis, football and billiards,
You will have ample time to do Sadhana.

Mind is very treacherous;
If you think when the alarm rings at 4 a.m.,
I will get up after ten minutes
You will never get up;
You will sleep till 8 a.m.

If you begin to take a few resins
When you fast on Ekadasi
The determination will slacken;
You will try to take some plantains, milk
Then two laddus, half a seer of milk etc.

Therefore be firm in your determination,
Come what may! stick, Be adamant,
Do not give a long rope to the mind,
Cut all temptations in one stroke.

2. DO INTEGRAL SADHANA

SADHANA must be integral and all-pervading;
Keep up the Divine Bhav during Vyavahara also,
Only then can you grow and evolve quickly.
Some roll the beads for one hour in the morning

INSTRUCTIONS ON SADHANA

And one hour at night;
They study one chapter of the Gita,
But during work they forget everything.

They quarrel and fight
They indulge in all sorts of sundry talks,
They do a little "gup shup" here,
And "gup shup" there,
They become victims of like and dislike.

They forget "All are manifestations of Lord."
They tell lies and hurt the feelings of others,
All good Samskaras are wiped out quickly,
By such conduct during work.

Again and again repeat the Name of the Lord
Feel His Presence everywhere
In all names and forms,
You will soon attain God-realisation.
Convert all work into Yogic activity.
Remember "work is worship of the Lord".
Vyavahara with the right Bhav is Pooja.
Remember the Sloka "Atma Tvam Girija Matih".

3. SONG OF SADHANA

(Thars: Sunaja)

RAMA Bhajo Rama Bhajo Rama Bhajo ji
Rama Krishna Govinda Gopala Bhajo ji.

I will try to learn one new thing every day,
I will do one good act daily, daily.

ANTARAI

I will practise Asanas daily to remove inertia,
I will do Suryanamaskar to get rid of lethargy.
I will practise virtues to make the mind positive,
I will never allow the mind to remain negative.
I will be ever diligent, vigilant and be on the alert,

I will march forward always to attain the goal of life.
                              Rama Bhajo...
I will never indulge in anything in which the
                              worldlings indulge,
I will not allow the mind to copy and imitate them.
I will try to become like Yudhishthira,
I will strive to tread the path which Buddha has trodden,
I will lead the life which Kabir, Nanak, Ram Das have led,
I will emulate Bhishma, Sankara and Guru Dattatreya.
I will remember the teachings of Lord Buddha
                              and Lord Mohammed,
I will practise the precepts of Lord Krishna
     and Vyasa Bhagawan.   Rama Bhajo...

I will not be careless and say "There is no danger",
I will not be heedless and say "I am perfectly safe",
I will try to fortify myself in all directions,
To resist the subtle workings of the mysterious Maya.
I will try to fence myself strongly and powerfully,
To resist the temptations and snares of Avidya.
                              Rama Bhajo...

I will not say in future "I will indulge in this
     just only once".
This "only once" will multiply into thousand and ones.
This "only once" will pull me down in the dark abyss,
This "only once" will cause in me hopeless downfa

I will never say 'by and by' and put off doing so.
Opportunities come but once and soon slip away.
Through the grace of the Lord and my adorable Guru,
I have now found out this clever Maya's trick.
I will do in future rigorous Tapas and meditation,
I will strengthen my resolves and hold Siva's Trisul.
                              Rama Bhajo...

4. TO THE SADHAKA

HAVE an open mind,
    A clean consciousness,
A noble character,
    A clear understanding of Truth,
A broad outlook of life,
    A new spiritual vision,
A good receptive mind,
    A loyal sense of duty to the Preceptor,
A childlike Svabhava,
    A willing obedience to saints,
A pure, melting heart for the distressed,
    A brave spirit to protect Dharma.

5. MAN WANTS COMFORTABLE SAMADHI

ONE man lies in his bed
He wants to catch the sky and the stars,
One man does a little Kumbhak
He wishes that the Kundalini must come to Sahasrara,
Another man does a little Japa
He wants to have vision of the Lord,
Another man lives on milk, fruits and buttermilk,
He wants to attain great Siddhis.

Another man studies a little of Upanishads
He wants to attain Brahma Jnana,
One man sits for a while on the banks of the Ganga
He wants to enter into Nirvikalpa Samadhi,
One man cuts his lower portion of tongue
He wants to fly in the air through Khechari.

No one wants to do rigorous meditation and Tapas,
But he wants Jivanmukti very quickly.
Self-realisation demands rigorous Sadhana,
Constant meditation and intense Tapas.

6. MARCH ON, HERO

RAISE not the voice when you are angry;
Look not on anybody with an angry look,
Do not utter harsh and vulgar words,
Be cautious, be cool, be serene.
Repeat the Name of the Lord silently,
Sing OM, chant OM, sing "Hare Rama",
Remember all forms are forms of the Lord,
Bow mentally to all beings with Narayana Bhav.
Again and again generate the Bhav,
Cultivate again and again Mithya Drishti,
Pray for inner strength and peace,
Cultivate Vichar and Brahma Bhavana,
Think of the evil results of anger and hatred,
And the benefits of love, kindness and mercy.
Remember hatred will rebound upon you,
With redoubled force and strength.
Bear in mind reaction follows an action.
Thus march on hero in the spiritual path,
And reach the goal, the immortal abode of bliss.

7. MARCH FORWARD, O FIERY SOLDIER!

O FIERY Adhyatmic soldier, march hero, march
With freedom song, with the song of OM;
Tarry not, reach the goal.
O spiritual knight!
Be brave, kill the enemies of peace—
Lust, anger, greed, selfishness and egoism.
Be firm in your rugged way, long and weary;
Look not back, march forward, march!
Come out victorious now;
Wear the laurels of eternal peace and bliss.
Hold your banner of immortality aloft.

8. SERVE AND BE DISPASSIONATE

HOWEVER much one may study Upanishads,
Brahma Sutras, Yoga Vasishtha,
Advaita Siddhi, Svarajya Siddhi,
Naishkarmya Siddhi, Brahma Siddhi,
Ishta Siddhi and other Siddhis,
Bliss and Realisation will never come,
Unless one is endowed with burning dispassion,
Strong yearning for liberation;
A pure, melting heart through selfless service;
Unless all worldly life, that seems to be real
Is not realised as untrue;
It is only fools that take
This world to be ever lasting and blissful.
For the sage there is no world;
For the discriminative it is all painful.

9. FOR WHOM IS THE WORLD UNREAL?

THIS world is unreal only for a Sage,
Who is above body-consciousness,
Who is resting in his own Svaroopa,
Who has identified with the all-pervading Brahman;
It is a solid reality for a passionate man.
It is the only reality for a greedy man;
For a Viveki or a man of discrimination,
With dispassion, self-restraint,
There is world
But it will not exert any influence.
But nowadays he who has studied a little Yoga
Vasishtha and Gaudapada Karika
Says "There is no world in the three periods of time";
But he is terribly afraid of a scorpion.
He trembles when he sees a cat at night.
He cannot take his food,
When there is less salt in dhall.
He cannot drink his tea

When there is less sugar.
He cannot bear a little insult or harsh word.
He must cover with sweater and blanket,
Even when there is a little cold.
Such a man is a downright hypocrite.
Believe not such a man.
In the three periods of time
He is terribly worldly.

10. WAY TO BEATITUDE

YOU cannot attain final beatitude
By mastering a million scriptures,
By practising rigorous austerities.
Brahman can only be realised
When all Vasanas and Trishnas perish,
When word ceases and thought dies,
When the veil of ignorance is rent asunder,
When the mind is absorbed in its source,
When the senses are curbed in toto,
When the Brahmakara Vritti rises,
Through constant Nididhyasana
And through the Grace of the Guru.

11. GOOD LIFE

DRINK not, smoke not,
Eat not meat and fish;
Abuse not, slander not, vilify not,
Injure not, utter not falsehood,
Waste not time in idle gossiping.
Be pure, be kind, be humble,
Be good, do good,
Be moderate in everything;
Serve, love, give,
Restrain, subdue the senses,
Cultivate divine virtues;

INSTRUCTIONS ON SADHANA

Do Japa, do Kirtan, meditate—
This is verily the good life.

12. SPIRITUAL APPETISERS

THE sight or memory even
Of lemon or ginger-pickles or chillies
Causes intense salivation.
They are all good stomachic appetizers—
You take more food.
Salivation goads the stomach
To secrete more gastric juice.
Even so the sight of Himalayas and Ganga,
Sadhus, Sannyasins, Bhaktas and Yogis,
Company of Sages and Mahatmas,
A good library, secluded places,
Himalayan retreats and caves,
Good spiritual books, Satsanga,
Study of the lives of saints,
Rosaries and deer skins,
Kirtan, Svadhyaya, holy places—
Are all spiritual appetizers.
They goad you to sit, meditate,
Introspect and do intense Sadhana.

13. WAY TO CONTROL THE SENSES

I DO not allow the tongue to speak evil of others;
I make it sing the glory of the Lord.
I do not allow the ears to hear scandals;
I make them hear sweet Kirtans.
I do not allow the eyes to run hither and thither;
I make them see the image of the Lord.
I do not allow the nose to smell scents;
I make it smell Tulasi and Bael leaves.
I do not allow the hands to do evil deeds;
I use them in the service of saints.
I do not allow the feet to go to any place;

I make them perambulate round the temple.
Use the sense, but do not abuse or misuse.

14. STORY OF TONGUE

THE tongue is in a danger zone;
It lies between the sharp teeth,
It is sharper than the sword;
One single word cuts others severely.
The wound remains till the end of life.
It has triple function,
It is an organ of knowledge;
It tastes eatables;
It is an organ of action also.
It is the organ of speech.

It has the sense of touch also;
Its end is full of nerves
Hence it is difficult to control this organ.
It is most mischievous and turbulent.
Control of tongue means control of all organs.
It excites the organ of reproduction,
Because both are born of the same Tanmatra;
They are sisters.
It teaches that one should be "Asanga"—
Any amount of ghee will not make it greasy.
Glory to that Saint who has controlled the tongue.

15. HARD IT IS TO KNOW

HARD, hard, hard it is to know the Self,
When lust, greed, anger and jealousy,
Attachment, egoism, conceit and cruelty
Are not destroyed in toto.
Difficult; difficult, difficult it is to attain Samadhi
When the heart is not purified by selfless service,
When the mind is not rendered steady by worship,
When the Grace of the Guru is not obtained.

INSTRUCTIONS ON SADHANA

Impossible, impossible, impossible it is to attain
                                     God-realisation
When one's ego asserts at every step,
When the senses hiss again and again,
When there are sex-attraction, sex-impulse and Vasanas.
Therefore root out egoism, and Vasanas first;
Discipline the senses; serve and serve;
Cultivate divine Virtues;
Do Japa, Kirtan; enquire, meditate!

16. KALPANA

THERE is only woman in this world:
Some one calls her "my sister",
Another calls her "my aunt"—
A third calls her "my niece"—
This is Kalpana.

There is only wood in this world:
Some calls it "my chair",
Another calls it "my table",
A third calls it "my desk"—
This is Kalpana.

It is Kalpana that binds you;
Kalpana is false imagination
Due to Avidya or ignorance.
Meditate and kill Kalpanas
And rest in Peace of the Eternal.

17. WATCH THE KALPANA

WATCH the Kalpana in the mind;
Stand as a witness or Drishta—
Identify not with the waves,
Hear not the voice of the mind,
Yield not to the mind's temptations;
Raise the rod of Viveka,
Draw the sword of dispassion—

Be calm, steady and serene.
All the waves will subside;
You will now swim freely
In the ocean of Brahmic Bliss;
Lord Yama will take to his heels.

18. O BISCUIT, IT IS LUXURY!

IN THE beginning of Sadhana period
Strict dietetic discipline is necessary,
But do not make too much fuss in diet;
Eat anything that comes by chance,
Suka Deva was starving for a week
At the gate of Janaka's palace.
Later on he was fed with dainties
By the Maharanis inside the palace.
He did not say:
"O biscuit is luxury! O mango is luxury!
O I have given up sugar and salt"
He ate whatever that was offered.
He had equanimity of mind.
This is wisdom.

New aspirants make much fuss in diet.
"O this is Tamasic; that is Rajasic;
This is luxury; that is Sattvic"
Their whole Sadhana ends with this only.
Householders eat with avidity.
They ever think and plan of palatable dishes.
But Sadhus think "When will they leave me?"
Two eyes, two ears, five fingers, two hands
Thirty-two teeth are all luxuries only.
One eye, three fingers, one hand,
Sixteen or eighteen teeth are sufficient.

19. "AHAMTA" AND "MAMATA"

MAN is bound by "Ahamta" and "Mamata",
"Ahamta" is I-ness, "Mamata" is mine-ness,

INSTRUCTIONS ON SADHANA

These are the two weapons of Maya,
Remove Ahamta and Mamata.
You will become one with the Absolute.

Jada Bharata had Mamata in the deer,
A dog or a monkey has Mamata in its tail,
A Mahant or a Baron has Mamata in his pot-belly,
A woman has Mamata in her dress, ornaments and hair.

A Sannyasin has Mamata in his Kamandalu and Ashram,
A grandpapa has Mamata in his grandson,
A police-man has Mamata in his moustache and stick,
An M.L.A. has Mamata in his "Rai Bahadur" title.

Mamata assumes various forms,
This is a trick of mind and Maya.

Maya spares not anybody in this world,
But she is afraid of a sage, Virakta and Viveki,
Therefore attain discrimination, dispassion and wisdom.

20. FIVE TRUNKS IN THE BODY

THE five Koshas are the five trunks.
Just as there is attachment for the trunks,
So also there is attachment for the Kosha-trunks.
In reality there is intense attachment for the Kosha-trunk;
You can abandon easily attachment to external trunks;
But it is difficult to renounce attachment to Kosha-trunks;
The attachment to external trunks has come
                              within a few years
But the Kosha-trunk attachment is from
                              beginningless time.
You cannot destroy the Svaroopa of the Koshas;
But you can develop the state of Asangata
                              and Nirabhimanata,
Through enquiry, dispassion and discrimination.
The physical body remains even for a sage;
There are hunger and thirst for him
But he has no attachment for the body;

And the Pranamaya Kosha,
As he identifies with the all-pervading Brahman.
Understand this salient point well
And be peaceful and joyful.

21. METHOD OF COMBINATION

ALL householders cannot renounce the world;
They will have to do Sadhana in the morning.
They can do Japa and Kirtan at night.
Even in the office they can write Mantra,
They can study a little Gita.
They can roll the beads in the pocket,
Every now and then they can repeat "HARI OM",
"Sri Ram", "Sita Ram", "Radheshyam".
They can feel: "The office is Brindawan,"
"All beings are manifestations of the Lord".
Give up 'Gup Shup' and idle talk;
Utilise every second in Nam Smaran.
Visualise the image of the Lord now and then.
You also can realise God amidst work.

22. METHOD OF CONVERSION

IF YOU find it difficult to do this even,
Adopt the "method of conversion".
Follow the teachings contained
In the verse "Atma Tvam Girija Matih ....."
Convert all works as offerings unto the Lord.
Let your sleep be your Samadhi.
Let your walk be perambulation.
Let all your speech be praise of the Lord.
Let all your sensual enjoyments be worship of the Lord.
Let your food be offering unto the Lord.
Say: "Om Tat Sat—Brahmarpanamastu"
"Krishnarpanamastu" "Ramarpanamastu".
Repeat the Sloka:
"Yatkaroshi Yadasnasi Yajjuhoshi Dadasi Yat;

Yat Tapasyasi Kaunteya Tat Kurushva Madarpanam."
And "Kayenavacha Manasendriyairva
            Buddhyatmanava Prakriter Svabhavat,
Karomi Yat Yat Sakalam Parasmai
            Sriman Narayanayeti Samarpayami."
You can also attain God-realisation easily
By this unique method of conversion.

23. SECRET OF KARMA YOGA

ALL forms are forms of the Lord.
The Lord does all actions
Through the instruments of Man,
As each deserves.
Man is only Nimitta.
The Lord is very just and impartial.
Why do you judge then the men as good or bad?
Consider all the actions to be Lord's own
And become wise.
No atom, no leaf can move,
Without the sanction of the Lord.
Feel this always and remove egoism,
Kartritva and Bhoktritva Bhavas.
No action will bind you, O Ram!
This is the secret of Karma Yoga.

24. O WISDOM, THE SUPREME WEALTH!

O WISDOM! Consumer of thoughts, desires and ignorance;
The fire that burns Karmas and Vasanas.
O Supreme Silence (Maha Mauna)! Vedas' goal;
Where there are no sounds;
Where vibration and speed end;
Where quarrels and discussions terminate;
Jnanam, Jneyam, Jnana-gamyam;
Wisdom, the object of wisdom by wisdom to be reached;
There is no purifier like thee in this world,
Thou art the bestower of final beatitude;

Thou art my sole possession, supreme wealth now;
I laugh at the vanity of Emperors and Kings.

25. ALL WISDOM IS EVER WITHIN YOU

ALL wisdom is ever within you.
The Immortal Bliss is ever within you.
All good is ever within you.
All power is ever within you.
All peace is ever within you.
All wealth is ever within you.
You should know the way of attainment.
You must have the courage to get them.
You must acquire first the Four.
You must be friendly with the four sentinels.
You must have faith, aspiration and devotion.
You must have a pure heart,
A clean conscience, and irresistible will,
Fiery determination and tenacity of purpose.

26. TRUE LIFE

TRUE life is the inner life:
It is Self-realisation,
It is all sweet Silence—
Man's supreme Goal, Centre and Ideal.
It is the consciousness of the one whole,
It is harmony, peace and bliss,
It is the ocean of joy,
It is the fountain of felicity;
It is the supreme abode of Vishnu,
It is the immaculate seat of Brahmic splendour,
It is the Immortal Essence, "Raso Vai Sah"—
It is Sahaja Samadhi.

27. TEAR MAYA'S VEIL

VEDANTA proclaims in a thundering voice
"Tat Tvam Asi"—Thou art That!

Realise this and be free.
If you wish to attain freedom,
Rend asunder Maya's thraldom:
Nothing here is permanent.
Brahman alone is permanent.
When Maya's veil drops,
You will realise "I am Brahman".
Sivananda says:
Names and forms are unreal—
The One Essence alone that permeates all is real;
'I' ness' 'Mine'-ness is real bondage.
A liberated sage lives very peacefully;
He is mindless of heat, cold, praise and censure.

28. PLAY ON THE MIND-VINA

MIND is your Vina or the lute—
OM or Ram is the string.
Vibrate OM or Ram continuously,
Play on the mind-Vina harmoniously.
Hear steadily the music of the soul—
The divine Anahat, the song of silence.
The Supreme Raga-Ragini.
It will lull you to Divine ecstasy,
It will give you rapturous delight;
You will enter into Nirvikalpa Samadhi,
All the worldly sounds will be drowned now—
You will enjoy the bliss of Atma,
The sweet, supreme Harmony of oneness,
The inner Calm of soundless Silence,
Where there is neither two nor talk.

29. ORIGINAL SIN

THE wrong notion "I am the body"
Is the real, original sin—
That erroneous thought
Is the "Aham Vritti"

The little self-arrogating "I",
The little "bubble", the 'I' thought
In the ocean of pure Consciousness;
This one thought has wrought all mischiefs,
This one thought has multiplied
Into thousand-fold thoughts;
This one thought separated man
From Sat-chit-ananda Brahman;
This one thought is born of ignorance.
Sin is only ignorance,
Sin is only a mistake
Committed by the baby soul,
Annihilate this little ego
Through meditation on the whole.
This thought will not arise again.
You will become one with the Absolute.

30. ATTAIN PERFECTION

WIPE out Karma, the cause of pain.
Through Akarta Bhav and Sakshi Bhav.
Identify with the all-pervading Brahman.
Burn ignorance through Knowledge of Self,
And attain Perfection that yields bliss.
Realise the One which is Ocean of Joy,
Which is delightful happiness,
Which has neither beginning nor end,
Which is within and without,
Which is the source for everything,
Which is beyond Gunas, Nada, Bindu and Kala,
Which the mind cannot approach.

31. SEEK THE ETERNAL

LET go all perishable objects;
Seek that which is Eternal.
Annihilate the lust of the flesh;
Kill the lust of the eyes.

Be pure and free within.
Put all thy trust in the Lord.
When thou hast the Lord, thou art rich;
Thou hast all Divine Aisvaryas.
Draw your whole heart unto Him;
Merge thy mind in Him;
Merge thy will in the Divine Will;
Now abide in the Supreme Peace of the Eternal.

32. LIBERATION

STAND firm in that place
Where there is neither East nor West,
Neither day nor night.
Remain steady in that realisation.
Now the notions "I am here", "Thou art there",
"This is near", "That is far",
"Today is Sunday", "It is 4 a.m.",
"I", "He", "You", "She", "It"
Will come to an end.
Abide thou in the ocean of Immortal Bliss.
Now you are liberated from births and deaths.

33. THE ABODE OF THE PURE

YOU have learned that body and mind are not "I".
You have learned that Prana is not "I".
The world is unreal, thou hast understood.
Thou hast understood that Brahman alone is true.
Now meditate on the formula "I am Brahman".
Lose thyself and unite with Him,
Rest here peacefully and joyfully.
This is the proper place, the abode of the pure.
The land of Eternal Bliss, Supreme Joy and Peace,
The Immaculate Seat beyond darkness,
Beyond good and evil, virtue and vice,
Beyond Tattvas, Gunas, cause and effect.

34. HEAR, REFLECT AND MEDITATE

IF YOU say "Jessamine, Jessamine, Jessamine"
You cannot smell its sweet aroma.
If you repeat "fire, fire, fire",
It will not burn your mouth.
If you repeat "sugar, sugar, sugar",
It will not make your tongue sweet.
If you repeat "Ice, ice, ice",
It will not quench your thirst.
Even so if you repeat "Aham Brahmasmi",
You cannot become Brahman.
You must first equip yourself
With the four means of salvation.
You must sit at the lotus feet of Sadguru,
You must serve him wet with devotion,
You must hear the Srutis from him,
And then reflect and meditate.
Only then can you attain Self-realisation;
You can become Brahman.

35. NOW, AN APTAKAMA

OBTAIN the grace of the Lord.
Leave the Tattvas, lose the self,
Become purified, stand unified,
Plunge deep in the ocean of bliss!
Subdue the self, realise the Truth.
With egoism gone, with distinction lost,
Remain unified with Brahman.
Rest peacefully in joy Supreme.
There is nothing more to learn now.
You have obtained everything,
You have done everything.
You are now an Aptakama, Kritakritya.

36. AS YOU SOW, SO YOU REAP

CAN the body come without reason?
Can disease come without reason?
Can accidents come without reason?
Can loss of property come without reason?
Can happiness and grief come without reason?
As you sow, so you reap.
They are all the fruits of your actions in the past.
Raga-dvesha arose from Mithya-Jnana.
Through Mithya-Jnana you took the body as the pure Atma.
Through Raga-dvesha you did Karmas.
Through Karmas you took this body.
If you wish to get rid of pain and enjoy bliss,
Do not get a body and birth.
Get rid of birth
By attaining Knowledge of the Supreme State.

37. LISTEN, FRIEND!

LISTEN, listen to the cry of Siva:
Wage war with slavery and duality.
Tarry not, delay not, run, run fast.
Sing the song of Immortality
"Sivoham Sivoham Sivoham Soham
Satchidananda Svaroopoham".

Drink the immortal nectar of unity.
I entreat thee, friend, drink it now.
Atman is nearer to you than the nose.
Thou art an Emperor, do not beg.
Thou art ever full, free and perfect.

Thy splendour, glory and Light are ineffable.
Sing "OM Tat Sat, OM Tat Sat, OM Tat Sat OM,
OM Santi, OM Santi, OM Santi OM."

38. OPEN THE EYE OF YOUR HEART

OPEN the eye of your heart,
And enjoy the vision of the Lord.
Break the seal of your ego
And realise the eternal bliss of the Self.

Clean the dirt of your mind's mirror
And behold the beauty of the Majestic Atman.
Sit on the horse of Brahmakara-Vritti,
And reach your destination, the home of Eternal Peace.

Still the waves of the mind
And take a dip in the ocean of bliss.
Shut up your mouth and the mouth of the mind,
And enjoy the Peace of the Supreme Silence.

39. MERGING

YAMUNA merges in the Ganga at Prayag.
There is no more Yamuna now.
Rivers merge in the sea.
They lose their names and forms.
Even so the individual soul merges in Brahman.
It loses its name and form.
Merging in Nirvikalpa Samadhi of Kaivalya
Merging is Sadyomukti.
Merging in Brahman is the goal of life.
Merging is the Advaita realisation of oneness.
In merging mind melts like ice in Silence.
It is absorbed in its source.
A Bhakta does not want to merge himself.
He wants to keep up his individuality.
He wants to sit in the presence of the Lord.
He wants to eat the sugarcandy.
He does not want to become sugarcandy itself,
Like the Advaita Vedantin or Jnana Yogin.
He too in the end merges himself.

Mira merged herself in Lord Krishna.
Merging is the highest Realisation.

40. THE DAY OF FULL ILLUMINATION

WHEN I rest peacefully in my Satchidananda Svaroop,
When the tempting world vanishes for me in toto,
When Deha-adhyasa disappears totally,
When my mind is balanced in pleasure and pain,
When I experience equal vision,
When censure and praise torment me not,
When egoism, likes and dislikes are destroyed,
When all cravings and desires leave me,
When I behold Brahman only everywhere,
When I am above good and evil,
When I do not feel pain when my leg is cut,
When I forget all about the world,
The day when these do happen is the day
Of my full illumination or Poorna Brahma-Jnana,
When painful birth and death will cease.

41. THREE OBSTACLES

VISHAYASAKTI is an obstacle in meditation,
It is intense clinging to mundane objects,
The mind again and again thinks of objects,
It remembers about old enjoyments.

Study Durga Sapta Sati,
The Vaisya who was driven by his wife,
Again and again remembered her and children,
The king had memories of his past life.

A dull intellect is another obstacle,
It cannot do enquiry and meditation,
It slips into old ruts and sleeps,
It cannot grasp the subtle truths.

The third obstacle is Vipareetha Buddhi,
A perverted intellect views things in a wrong manner,

It takes the unreal for real and vice versa,
It takes the body as Atma or Real Self.

It thinks "there is nothing beyond sensual pleasure".
Satsanga, service and Kirtan will remove the three obstacles,
Therefore live with sages, serve and do Kirtan.

42. WHIMS OF SADHAKAS

SOME concentrate their Sadhana on hair
Some apply ash and make it golden
Some shave the head completely
Some keep Jata or matted hair
Some keep long hair
Some have 'modified crop'
They all have their hair
Under perfect control.

Some have long beard
They apply oil and comb it daily
They think that a beard
Will give a good personality,
Make them appear saintly and Yogily
And bring respect from all quarters.

This is their hair (or *Mayir*) Sadhana,
This mind assumes hair-akara Vritti,
Their minds are ever fixed on hair.
This is their goal, centre and ideal.
They make the body Brahman or a saint.
They cheat themselves and others too.

Their hands are ever on their beard.
Watch carefully, you will agree with me.

II

Some do Kowpeen or Langot Sadhana,
Today they will wear Gerua gown or orange Alpee
Tomorrow they will put on

INSTRUCTIONS ON SADHANA

A short cloth above the knee;
Next day they will have only one Kowpeen.
The following day they will roam about stark naked
They think they have realised the Avadhut state
Of possessionlessness and perfect non-attachment.

But the mind remains in the same state or even worse state
Because their egoism is intensified now.
Their veil of ignorance is thickened
By this sort of Tapas.
They think that they are superior Sadhakas.

III

Now comes neem-leaves-buttermilk Sadhana,
Some live on neem leaves for a month
Some drink cow's urine
Some leave salt and sugar
They take buttermilk today
They live tomorrow on vegetables
They live next day on groundnut
They live the following day on Sattu
They observe Mauna but say 'Ha', 'Hu', 'Hm, 'O'
They talk more than a worldly man,
Cultivate 'Mitha Bhashana,' little useful talking.

IV

Next comes Sadhana in Himalayas
Some live in Gangotri,
Some live in caves,
Some live in Uttarakasi,
Some live in lonely forests,
Some live in Mount Kailas,
Some live in Mansarovar,
They think they have realised Brahman.

V

But their nature remains the same
Or becomes worse even
On account of a little Tapas Abhimana,
Their quarrelling and arrogant nature
Becomes more marked,
Their egoism is more hard than granite,
They wander about advertising
That they are Jivanmuktas,
They repeat Sivoham Soham,
Little things upset them
And make them "Durvasas",
They now begin to start "Ashrams"
And open "Dharma Sanghas"
To do Lokasangraha.

VI

Taking neem, remaining naked, keeping beard
Is the gist of their whole Sadhana.
Their Sadhana ends with these only,
They think of buttermilk, beard, Kowpeen,
                              cave and Gangotri.
Due to mal-nutrition and exposure,
They contract chronic diseases
And die an early unnatural death,
They miss their life's goal,
They never think of the Eternal.

This is all due to their 'Manmukh nature',
They have not done any 'Gurumukh Sadhana'
By living under a Guru.

VII

Keeping a beard cannot make one a Jnani,
Eating neem leaves cannot make one a Yogi,
Giving up salt cannot open the Kundalini,
Salt, sugar and cloth are not obstacles to Brahma Jnana;
Kings were in possession of Brahma Jnana.

INSTRUCTIONS ON SADHANA

Remaining naked cannot make one an Avadhoot,
Purify the mind, reduce the egoism to zero
Live under a Guru and practise Sadhana
Serve the poor, regenerate the Asuric nature
Eat anything that comes by chance
Do not make any show of your saintliness.

Be steady, firm, normal and uniform
Abandon eccentricity and queer nature,
Never give up selfless service,
Do not jump to the skies at once,
Shave the mind and burn the Vasanas and Dambachariness,
Be mentally silent and yet dynamic
And waft the divine aroma everywhere.

Hari Om, Sri OM, Siva OM, Ram OM.

Chapter VI

MIND AND ITS CONTROL

1. TO THE MIND

O TRUANT mind! O mischievous imp!
I am tired of giving you admonitions.
You are like the strolling street dog;
The dog is pelted with stones,
And beaten with shoes severely;
And yet it again goes to the doors of people.

You are like the shameless son-in-law
Who sits idly in the house of his father-in-law,
Eats and drinks, bearing all rebukes and broom-beatings!

It is difficult to control the turbulent mind
Without the Grace of the Lord;
The Prompter of the thought alone
Can subjugate this wild mind.
My prostrations and adorations to the Prompter!

2. LISTEN, O MIND

LISTEN, O mind, this last piece of advice.
Sink not in bonds, in mire of Samsara.
In the perilous ocean of births and deaths,
Mix thou not in mundane affairs.
Eat not the fruits of pain and sorrow.
Take not birth again and again.
Wither not thyself in wicked deeds.
Is not eternal bliss thy quest?
Commune with the Lord of Bliss now.
Forget the body and its connections.
Rest peacefully in blissful joy.

MIND AND ITS CONTROL

Calmly abide in thy Supreme Abode.
Now there shall be an end of birth.

3. SOAR HIGH LIKE A KITE

REPEAT, O Mind! The Name of Hari.
Hari's Name is a safe boat
To take you to the other shore of immortality.
Sing the Maha Mantra constantly:

HARE RAMA HARE RAMA
RAMA RAMA HARE HARE
HARE KRISHNA HARE KRISHNA
KRISHNA KRISHNA HARE HARE.
This is a triple-strong weapon
To cut the tie of Samsara certainly.
Soar high in the heaven like a kite.
Swim in the ocean of Bliss.

4. ROAM NOT, O MIND!

ROAM not, O mind!
In sensual objects.
Desire not for name, fame, prestige,
Position, titles, honours and rank.

Care not, O mind,
For earthly affection, love and kind words,
Respect, nice clothes and dainty dishes,
Company of damsels and their talks.
Remain steadfastly gazing on the Lord
Who dwells in the cave of the heart,
Thy refuge, solace, source and centre,
Witness, Abode, Lord and Dissolution.

5. MIND IS VERY TREACHEROUS

Mind is very treacherous;
It will hurl you down in the abyss of ignorance.
Peetva Peetva Punar Peetva Punar Janma na Vidyate—

Drink, again drink, there is no rebirth;
It will say "Give up Sadhana;
You will not gain anything;
There is no bliss beyond senses.
The world is real.
There is nothing like sensual pleasure.
Enjoy it to your heart's content."
Hear not the voice of the mind.
Swim against the mind current.
Mind is your bitterest enemy.
Bear this always in your mind.
Treat the mind as such.
Disconnect yourself from the mind.
Ever stand as its silent witness.
Do not become one with the mind and its Vrittis.
Ever introspect and practise self-analysis.
The mind will lurk as a thief.
It cannot do any havoc.
It will gradually be tamed.
It will become your obedient servant.

6. DO NOT CO-OPERATE WITH THE MIND

Sensual pleasures are nectar in the beginning;
But they are venom in the end.
Co-operate not with the mind.
This is the way to thin out the mind.
This is the method to control the mind.
If the mind says: "Go to cinema,"
Say to the mind: "I will attend the Sadhana Week,"
And immediately proceed to Ananda Kutir.
If the mind says: "Attend the nautch party,"
Take part in Akhanda Kirtan and Satsanga.
If the mind says: "Eat eggs, meat,"
Eat spinach, fruits and milk.
If the mind says: "Read novels, newspapers,"
Study Gita, Upanishads and Practice of Karma Yoga.
If the mind says: "Take part in horse race,"

MIND AND ITS CONTROL

Go to Badri Narayan and Gangotri.
If the mind says: "Gamble in Deewali,"
Practise vigil and do Kirtan whole night.
If the mind says: "Go to the club for gossiping and card's play,"
Attend the Satsanga and do Japa intensely.

Chapter VII

PHILOSOPHY IN HUMOUR

1. SUNDAY NOW FRIDAY (GANDHI DAY)

SUNDAY is a happy day;
Man takes rest, has no office work.
Now Friday will become a happy day.
He can play Bridge and physique.
He can drink, smoke and gamble.
Further he can have a decent shave.
The barber makes even an old man young!
After a shave he looks more bright.
He jumps, dances, walks with high steps.
His gait changes; he often looks at the mirror.
Too many people gather round the barber.
There is quarrel about the seniority.
Vaman applies soap himself first
In order to be the senior candidate.
But Raman who came first
Raises his fist against Vaman.
One can enjoy the fun near Dharmashala.
O Man! Sunday is the best day for doing intense Sadhana.
Do more Japa, meditation and Kirtan,
Observe complete Mauna for 24 hours.
If you are earnest, if you do rigorous Sadhana,
You can realise even within 24 hours.
Waste not time in "gup" "shup";
And do not make this precious life "dawa-dhole",

2. DO YOU KNOW THIS "I.C.S." AND "P.C.S."

ONE man puts his title as M.Bh.
This is not a doctor's title,
It means only "Madras Brahmin".

One man has his title S.S.O.
It is not a sub-divisional officer,
It means, "simply sitting officer"
That is an idler, loafer or a Faltu.

One man uses the title, M.R.K.D.
It means a "member of the
Rice killing department" or
"Rotti killing department"
That is a glutton or Sapat-raman
Who fills his belly with rice or Rotti upto mouth.

Another calls himself I.C.S. in summer
And P.C.S. in winter,
It means Ice Cream Seller in summer
And Potato Chop Seller in winter.

Such title holders are plenty in this world.
Please do not aspire to own
Such big titles and come to lime light.

Shun all titles, hide yourself,
You will be peaceful.
Sincerity, simplicity, humility,
Generosity and devotion to God—
These you should own and not
Self-deluding and world-cheating titles
Of the above type.

3. A GREAT F.F.S. AND F.T.D.

ONE man applied for a Head Master's Post,
He has passed only third form,
But he put his title as F.F.S. F.T.D.

The Trustees of the High School
Were enamoured of his big titles,
They appointed him as the Head Master.

The Head Master worked for a week,
He was not able to deliver lectures,
The students pressed him to deliver lectures,
But the head master blinked.

The Trustees asked "What are these titles then?
You are not able to deliver lectures."
He said "I am Father of Five Sons, F.F.S.
And Father of Ten Daughters, F.T.D."

The trustees said "Get away at once,
On! cheat head master, we do not want you."

This world abounds with cheats.
Beware, be cautious, be vigilant,
Do not be carried away by titles, F.F.S. F.T.D.

America issues very cheap titles.
Egoistic man wants titles,
To pose as a big man in this world.
Be simple, humble, do not cheat.

4. TAMARIND BRAIN

MADRASEES have "Tamarind Brains".
Tamarind brains work wonders.
Ramanujam (Mathematician) had a tamarind brain.
Sir S. Radhakrishnan is also a tamarind brain.
Sri Sankaracharya and Ramanuja had tamarind brains.
Subramania Bharathiar also is a tamarind brain.
There is a special mysterious Vitamin in tamarind.
It is "Brain Vitamin X Y Z".
It is also known as "Tamiro-Vigorine".
It energises the Pineal and Pituitary glands.
It beautifully sharpens the intellect;
Excels Lecithin, phosphorus and yolk of eggs;

Gives vigour to the brain cells;
Bestows acumen, wisdom, discrimination,
And makes one a genius or prodigy.
Glory to Tamarind and "Tamarind brains".

5. WHO IS "A-1 LOOF" IN SIRSHASAN

HE is a confirmed fool,
If he throws the diamond and takes a broken glass piece,
He is a first class dunce,
If he throws the butter
And runs for the ghee in the market.

He is a A-1 'loof' in Sirshasan,
If he leaves "Ananda Kutir"
And goes to the town for getting peace.

He is a capital dullard,
If he leaves "Ram Nam"
Which bestows, eternal bliss and immortality,
And runs after useless earthly objects.

He is indeed dull-witted
If he leaves the company of saints and Ganga,
And goes back to Bombay again to do business,
Or joins again the office with hat and boot,
And signs "your most obedient servant"
And does Japa of "yes, sir, very well sir, ji huzur".
He is the most wretched man on this earth,
Shun his company at all times.

6. "KHOON KHARAB HOGAYA"

WHEN the blood is full and thick
The young man jumps and dances;
Twists his moustache and denies God.
It is all "I did this" "I know everything"
"No one is equal to me" "I can do anything".

He drinks, gambles, plays all mischief.
Gets various sorts of diseases;
Then comes to the doctor and says:
"Doctor Sahib Khoon Kharab Hogaya,"
And takes '606' and '914' injections.

His face is pale now.
He walks with tottering steps,
He hides his face in shame,
He drags a cheerless existence.

O Man! when you are full blooded
Think of God, be good and do good,
Walk in the path of righteousness,
Approach the saints and follow their instructions,
You will reap a rich harvest of peace.

7. SOLVE THIS RIDDLE, PLEASE!

YOU came once;
And then went away;
Then again you came;
And then went away:
Now you will not come any more—
What is this?
If you cannot solve this riddle,
I shall give you the answer—
It is "teeth".
They came once as milk-teeth;
And then went away.
Then they came as permanent teeth.
They all fall when you become old:
They will not come any more.

But Brahman never comes nor goes:
It always exists.
Attain this toothless Brahman through meditation;
And become Immortal!

8. THE GREATEST MISER

IN Manasic Pooja or mental worship,
You can offer anything to the Lord.
You can offer the sweetmeats of the whole world,
The fruits of the entire universe,
The gold and rubies of all mines,
The clothes of the whole world;
But one devotee offered in his mental worship
One stale plantain only and one teaspoonful of
                                    green gram only!
Is he not the greatest miser?
If he is such a sort of miser even in mental offering
                                    to the Lord,
How can one expect even a grain of rice from him?
He will not give even a little salt to a man with a
                                    cut in the finger.
He will not drive the crows when he is taking food
Because a grain of rice might fall on the ground
Which the crow might get!
Such misers are burden on this earth.
O man! Develop a generous heart,
Give, give, give, always give.
This is the secret of abundance.
You will inherit the whole wealth of the Lord.
You will be ever full.
Dhana Lakshmi, Dhanya Lakshmi will ever dwell in you.

9. FREAKS OF NATURE

SOME coconut trees bifurcate at the top.
There are coconuts at both tops.
Some coconut trees bear fruits
When they are four feet above the ground.
A goat has two udders in the neck
Which give abundant milk.
Twins are united at the sides.
Each segment of a tapeworm

Contains sexual organs of both kinds
And gets self-impregnated.
A hermaphrodite is an individual
In whom are united the properties of both sexes.
If man also can get self-impregnated like the tapeworm,
What will become the fate of these women?
Then they will have to pack themselves to
                                        another plane or colony.
Then all the Home Ministers will have tight work
For a couple of years in arranging for their "visas".
Maya is an illusory power of the Lord.
She can do any number of freaks.
She can create a cool sun and a hot moon!
A sage knows fully well all Her tricks.
There is nothing astonishing for him.
Maya hides Herself before him in shame.
Because he has found out Her tricks!

10. TIRUPATI SHAVING

IN Tirupati a barber is very busy.
His clients are countless.
Children and elders shave their heads;
This is considered very auspicious.
The barber shaves a little portion first.
He does not want to lose his client.
He collects a large number,
Then he begins to shave one by one neatly.

A tailor, even when he has very tight work,
Will not refuse to undertake the work of anybody.
He will simply collect work from all corners,
And will give lame excuses daily.
When he sees a man,
He will pretend to take up the work;
And cut a small portion and stitch.
When the man leaves his shop,
He will take up another work.

Even so some take up my letters;
After five or six days, say
"I have kept the reply on the table,
Yes, Narayanaswami has taken that letter;
No, no, it is with Premananda,
No, no, it is with Atma Ram in the Post Office."
In reality the letter is somehow lost.
Be not like the barber or tailor.
Take up any work, and finish it promptly.
Give not this and that lame excuse.
Stick to your promise.

11. "UPPUMA-COFFEE" IS SWEETER THAN BRAHMAN!

A MADRASI says:
"Your Brahman is not so sweet
As my uppuma, sambar and coffee."

A Maharashtrian says:
"Your Atman is not so delicious
As my Varan, Amte and Pooranpoali".

A Punjabi declares:
"Your Vedantic Brahman is not so palatable
As my Parotta, milk and sag."

A Gujarati says:
"Your Upanishadic Atman is not so sweet
As my kadhi, laddu and tea."

A Bengali asserts:
"Your Brahman is not so delicious
As my Rasagulla and Sandesh."

A European proclaims:
"Your Brahman is not so sweet
As my beef-steak, sweet pudding and dripping."

Maya is very powerful.
It deludes, tricks and dupes.

It makes unreal appear as real
And hides the Real.
Maya makes the objects appear
More sweet than Brahman
In order to deceive the worldlings.
Any amount of lecturing and tuition
Cannot open the eyes of these people.
They are immersed and soaked in worldliness 1001 deep!

Pain, deep and continuous knocks of this world,
Satsanga, discrimination and enquiry,
At last open their eyes.
They act as wisdom collyrium.

12. STORY OF AN APPLICANT

"MOST Honoured Sir,
I appeared for Matriculation Examination six times;
But unfortunately got plucked.
This is my qualification.
My parents are penniless, many children,
Poor condition, "pillai kutti plenty";
Dharma Doraithan Rakshikanum—
Your Lordship only should protect me.
I cannot continue my study.
Being given to understand
That there is a vacancy in your Honour's Office,
I apply myself as a candidate for the same.
Please confer this post on me.
For this act of charity
I, as in duty bound, pray
For your Honour's long life, prosperity and posterity.
Your most obedient servant,
A. R. Krishnaswamy,
72-A Muthu Ramalinga Street,
Vepery, Madras."

O Ignorant Youth! O slave! Why do you knock
At the doer of these petty officers
With such a pitiable deplorable, attitude?
Knock at the door of the Supreme King of kings
Who abides in the chambers of your heart.
Do Kirtan. Sing His Name. Repeat "Sri Ram".
You will attain all the wealth of the world
Plus the spiritual inexhaustible wealth of the Lord.
Thou art That—"Tat Tvam Asi."

13. ODE TO LADDU

O LADDU! O Sweet Laddu!
Adorations unto thee!
Thou art the pet child of Maya;
You delude the people to a great degree.

Children dance in joy when they look at you;
Even old people jump and whistle.
Last night the Bhajan Hall
Was packed with people
Because there was Laddu Prasad.

Jilebi, Peda, Rasagulla, Kalakand,
Are thy amiable companions;
But people like you only most.
I do not know what charms are in thee!

This world will be a void minus thee.
You hold a very prominent position
In Bhandaras, feasts and dinners.
Even Diabetics fill their stomachs with Laddus
On the strength of Insulin.

Thou art very dear to Mathura Chaubeys.
Even Dysenteric patients cannot leave thee;
They do not mind aggravation of the disease.

You are only a modification of mud and water;
And yet how powerful thou art!

You hold sway over all,
You put down your head in shame
Before sages, devotees and Yogis,
Because they know your hollowness.

Goodbye, Laddu amiable comrade!
Continue thy work vigorously
And delude the worldly weaklings intensely.

14. U. N. O.

(This is in Lake Success, New York)

Ultimate Nameless Ocean of Bliss
Ulterior Nectarine Oasis
Ultra Nerveless One without a second,
Ultra sensual Nescienseless Overseer
Ultra mundane Newsless Outsideless Brahman
Unadulterate Numberless Omniscience
Unaffected Noumenon Oversoul
Unalloyed Noiseless Oneness
Unalterable Nirvana Ocean of Joy
Unattached Not-this Not-this Ocean of Peace.
But this wonderful U. N. O is in countryless
                                        Niralamba Puri,
Become a member of this U. N. O. now.
No fees, no degrees but possess the four V. V. S. M.

Chapter VIII

BHAKTI AND SELF-SURRENDER

1. PRAISE BE TO THE LORD

PRAISE be to the Lord, the Creator,
The Omniscient, Omnipotent and Omnipresent,
The Merciful, the Compassionate,
The Inner Ruler of all beings!
Supervisor, Permitter, Prompter,
Supporter, Enjoyer, Indweller,
Source of all beings, Lord of all beings,
The Supreme Abode and Treasure-house!
Shelter, origin, foundation and dissolution,
Infinite, Eternal, Unborn, Undecaying,
Immortal, Blissful and Unconditioned,
Self-existent, Self-contained and Self-luminous!

2. A PRAYER

O ADORABLE Lord of Compassion!
At dawn when the glorious sun
Dispels the darkness,
Grant me strength and concentration
To meditate on Thee.
Throughout the day
Let me serve the humanity
With love, kindness and Atma-bhav.
Let me remember Thee at all times;
Let me not deviate a bit
From the path of righteousness or Dharma;
Let me be established in Brahma Nishta.
Let me be endowed with non-attachment,

Discrimination, serenity and courage;
At night let me again meditate on Thee
With full strength, vigour and Bhav.
Let me sleep in Thy arms, O Lord!

3. THIS IS MY PRAYER, O LORD!

O LORD Hari! Protector of this World!
Kill my egoism and Abhimana;
Make me desireless and angerless;
Let me behold Thee in all Forms;
Let me see Thee within and without;
Let me be ever attached to Thy Lotus Feet;
Let me ever sing Thy name and Glory;
Let me serve the saints and sages;
Let me not see any defect in any one.
Let me be endowed with equal vision;
Let me ever have equanimity of mind;
Let me ever dwell in the company of saints;
Let me have unswerving faith in Thee and Thy Name
Even if my throat is cut.
Sow the seed of Creeper of Love in my heart,
This is my fervent prayer, O Lord Hari.
Grant me this prayer;
I am suppliant to Thee.

4. SURRENDER AND BE AT EASE

IS THERE not a Lord to protect all beings?
Is He not Omnipotent and Omniscient?
Is He not Compassionate and Merciful?
Has He not saved Dhruva, Prahlada,
Ajamila, Mira, Surdas, Tulasi and others?
Why covet, wrangle and worry, O Man?
Whatever must come, of itself will come.
God does everything for your own good.
He is just and knows everything.
He knows what is good for you.

BHAKTI AND SELF-SURRENDER

You do not gain anything by worrying.
Why do you carry the load on your head even when
                              you are in the train?
Surrender thyself at His Lotus Feet,
And be at ease, like the man
Who kept his load on the train.
The Lord will take care of you.

5. MOST PERFECT FOOD

YOU cannot live on bread alone,
You cannot live on daal and milk alone,
You cannot live on fruits and vegetables alone,
You cannot live on vitamin extracts alone;
But you can live on Name of God alone.

You can attain Immortality through Lord's Name;
Name is the most powerful food,
Name is the food of all foods,
Name is the most well-balanced diet.

The food-Name is available at all times;
This is the most potent, cheapest and best.
This Name immortalised Prahlada and Dhruva.
It was food and drink to Mira and Tulasidas.

Sivananda says:
There is neither control nor famine for this;
Say "Goodbye" to all food controllers—
Turn your mind towards the Supreme Controller.
Eat this celestial food freely
And be blissful for ever.

6. THE INNER RULER

THE Lord dwells within and ever prompts.
He is the silent witness and supervisor.
He is the Inner Ruler or Antaryamin.
He illumines the mind and the senses.
He gives power to the intellect and the organs.

He moves the mind and the senses.
He is the "Light of lights" in the heart,
And yet they have not found Him out,
Because their mind is outgoing;
It is filled with cravings and desires;
It is not tamed and disciplined;
It is gross, impure and vascillating;
It is screened by the veil of ignorance.

7. LOVE—A MIGHTY POWER

LOVE is a mighty power!
It speaks louder than words.
It is the greatest power on this earth.
It is a great cementing force.
It grones from one's pure heart.
It is a soothing divine balm.
It heals, unites and blends;
It redeems and saves;
It wins all hearts;
It penetrates and percolates.
Love melts into wisdom in the end.
Two have become one now.

8. THE LORD RUNS A MILE

IF you move one foot to meet the Lord,
He will run a mile to receive you!
He is very kind and compassionate.
There is at your back His Hand
To protect you at all times.
Place thy trust in Him for support;
Feel His hidden Hand working
Through all sources.
Surrender your ego at His Feet;
And be at ease for ever!

BHAKTI AND SELF-SURRENDER

9. THE SUPREME MEDICINE

IS THERE any foe except the mind?
Is there any shelter except the Lord?
Is there any help except His Grace?
Is there any friend except the Indweller?
Is there any benefactor except the Inner Ruler?
Is there any Emperor except the Almighty?
Is there any Doctor except Lord Narayana Hari?
Is there any medicine except His Name?

10. NAME IS NECTAR!

SING "Hare Rama Hare Rama Rama Rama Hare Hare;
Hare Krishna Hare Krishna Krishna Krishna Hare Hare,
Cry "Hari! Hari!!"
It is very easy to utter it.
Let the honey-sweet Name dwell for ever on thy lips,
Let the Name ever ring in your ears,
It is the path to achieve Life's Goal;
Fetters of duality cannot bind you now.
You will gain great merit and peace!
Name of the Lord is Nectar of Immortality.
Name will save you from birth and death.
You will attain lustre and Joy.

11. DRINK THIS CELESTIAL AMBROSIA

THERE is a mysterious Bhuti or celestial herb,
The herb that immortalises
And transforms man into Divinity;
A beverage made out of this Bhuti
Is most delicious and invigorating.
It is the "Hari Nam" Bhuti.
It is the Name of the Lord.
Mira drank this Bhuti-elixir day and night.
Hafiz was very fond of this cooling drink.
Tulasidas and Surdas drank this several times daily.

It was the daily food of Samarth Ram Das.
Dhanna Bhagat enjoyed this like anything.
Hanuman and Prahlad were intoxicated by this drink.
O Man! Drink this ambrosia to your heart's content,
And attain Immortality and Eternal Bliss.

12. PANACEA FOR BIRTH AND DEATH

MAKE your heart as the mortar,
When you prepare this celestial drink;
Rub the mortar with the pestle of "Sri Ram",
Rub it again and again forcibly;
Crush the cravings and "I-ness" and "mine-ness".
Sing or chant "Om Sri Ram Jaya Ram Jaya Jaya Ram".
Let the current be unbroken.
Add the syrup of meditation of Lord's Form;
Also add a few black pepper of "Grace" through surrender.
Now drink this elixir very freely.
Repeat it again and again.
This is the panacea for birth and death.

13. DRINK SIVAJNANAMRITAM

APPROACH the mighty King of Mount Kailas
Adorned with crescent moon, Ganga
And garland of skulls of His devotees;
The Store-house of wisdom and power,
Bestower of Immortal Bliss,
Who ever dwells in your heart,
Who is called Rudra, Bhava,
Hara, Sankara, Sambhu, Sadasiva,
Mahadeva, Neelakantha, Ponnambalam.
Sing at His Gate
"Om Namah Sivaya, Om Namah Sivaya"
And shed tears of Prem, wet with Bhakti.
He will speedily open the door
And feed you with the Immortal Nectar
"Siva Jnanamritam", or honey of wisdom.

14. PHILOSOPHY OF STONE IMAGE

I MADE a stone image of Lord Krishna
And worshipped the stone image with devotion.
The stone image is not Lord Krishna;
But my worship reached Lord Krishna.
The stone remains the stone it was;
The Lord looks into my Bhav,
My heart, motive and aspiration.
The stone image serves as a prop
To fix the mind on the Lord.
I felt the Presence in the stone image.
I recognised the Indweller or Inner Ruler.
When I grow in devotion,
The image talks, guides and inspires.
The stone image is part or body of Virat.
There is no such thing as dead-matter.
Everything is consciousness.
O ignorant man!
Understand well the philosophy of stone image,
And become wise and happy.

15. HOW COMPASSIONATE IS THE LORD!

LORD Rama installed his friend Vibhishana on the throne;
But he gave Mukti to his enemy Ravana
Who carried away His consort Sita.
He installed his friend Sugriva on the throne;
But he gave salvation to his enemy Vali.

Lord Krishna gave Mukti to his enemy Kamsa;
He gave salvation to Pootana
Who sucked Him with poison in her breast.

He gave Moksha to wicked Sisupala
Who abused and insulted him publicly.
Flee unto Him for shelter with all thy being.
By His grace thou shalt obtain supreme Peace;
The everlasting abode of eternal bliss.

16. GLORY TO THE FLUTE-BEARER

Who could know the path of devotion?
Who could know Siddhi and Mukti?
Who could know the essence of love?
Who could know the secrets of Prem,
Surrender, Grace, Rasa Lila and Gita?
If the Lord of Radha, Joy of Devaki,
Hath not come in the form with flute?

17. TEMPLE OF MY HEART

O LORD Hari, O Protector!
In the golden temple of my heart
Lit by the lamps of serenity and purity
I adore Thee daily.

The roof of the temple is devotion,
The pillars are self-surrender and faith.
I have decorated the temple
With the flowers of renunciation,
Dispassion and discrimination.

I burn the incense of Truthfulness
And wave the light of love.
Thy holy Name is the sweetest nectar.

Thou art my sole refuge—
I am Thine, I am Thine,
Thou art mine, Thou art mine,
Thus sayeth Sivananda.

18. MY VITTHALA PANDURANGA

My Lord Krishna!
My Radha Krishna!
Consort of Rukmini!
Beloved of Satya Bhama!
Let me live in Thee for ever.
        My Vitthala Panduranga!

Give me faith and devotion.
Love me as you loved the Gopis,
Arjuna, Uddhava and Sudama.
I have surrendered everything unto Thee—
My life, my mind, my heart, my soul, my all:
    My Murali Manohar!

Let me taste Thy secret love.
You cannot escape from my heart now.
I have tied You with the chord of love.
You are a thief who has stolen my heart.
You are Bhakta Vatsala,
Saranagata Vatsala, my Prananath.
    My Brindavan Bihari!

19. PRABHU MAHIMA STOTRA

O LORD! Thou art the greatest Mathematician,
Thou art the greatest Master, Architect and Engineer,
Thou art the greatest Doctor and Surgeon,
Thou art the Creator, Governor and Controller,
Salutations and Adorations unto Thee.

O Supreme Being! Thou art the greatest artist and songster,
Thou art the source of sound, Raga and Raginees,
Thou art colour, design, brush and drawing,
Thou art beauty, symmetry and rotundity,
Prostrations and obeisance unto Thee!

O Almighty! Thou art the beacon light and the guiding star,
Thou art the fountain head of joy and bliss,
Thou art the Supreme Treasure of treasures,
Thou art my prop, anchor and supporter,
Adorations and prostrations unto Thee,
Guide me; save me, enlighten me, O Lord!

20. TEACH ME, O LORD!

TEACH me to see beyond, O Lord!
To behold the One Self everywhere,

To go beyond body-consciousness,
To become thoughtless and cravingless!

Instruct me to cross over the three Gunas, O Lord!
To become a Sthitha Prajna or Gunatita,
To enter into Nirvikalpa Samadhi,
To get established in Nirdwandwa state.

Teach me to stand as the silent witness,
To see inaction in action and action in inaction,
To discriminate between real and unreal,
Right and wrong, good and evil.

Instruct me to fix the mind on Thee for ever,
To leave behind all names and forms,
Not to hurt others or to be hurt by others,
And to utilise the inner eye of intuition.

21. THOU ART THE JUST JUDGE

O ADORABLE Lord of Infinite Compassion!
Salutations unto Thee!
Thou art the best and just judge of my thoughts.
I believe Thou art the Prompter and witness.
Thou knowest the frailty and wickedness of men.
Thou knowest what I know not.
Forgive me whenever I am in the wrong.
Grant me Thy grace and inner strength.
Have pity on me, Thy servant.
I appeal to Thy mercy and grace only.
I do not claim "I am righteous"
By trusting on my frail conscience,
And the misguiding voice of my mind.
Thou knowest my heart much better.
Again adorations unto Thee, O Lord God!

22. DESCEND NOW O LIGHT

O FLOOD of joy! that cheered up Queen Mira
When she was tormented by Rana.

O torrent of bliss! that comforted Jesus
When he was crucified on the Cross.

O Supreme Peace that sustained Mansoor and
                                        Shams Tabreiz,
When they were tortured by the Badshaw.
O Sweet Celestial Honey! that energised boy Markandeya
When he was pulled by Lord Yama.

O Heavenly Manna! that sustained the life of Guru Govind
When he fought with his oppressors.
O Delightful Harmony! that encourages Sadhakas
When they are marching in the perilous razor path.

O Light of lights! that is ever burning
In the chambers of heart of all beings!
Descend now, fill my heart now,
Cheer me now, illumine me now.

23. O HIDDEN JOY!

O HIDDEN JOY! that removes all sorrows and sufferings,
O Hidden Nectar! that bestows Immortality,
O Hidden Light! that dispels the darkness of ignorance,
O Hidden Harmony! that removes all discords and strife,
O Hidden Peace! that destroys restlessness and disharmony,
O Hidden Bliss! that annihilates pain and grief,
O Hidden Knowledge! that destroys Avidya or Nescience,
O Hidden Love! that slays all hatred and jealousy,
Crores of salutations unto Thee, O Supreme Good!
Reveal Thyself unto me now and here.

II

O Hidden Felicity! that destroys all cares and worries,
O Hidden Beauty! that gives beauty to all forms,
O Hidden Freedom! that breaks all bondage,
O Hidden Eternal Satisfaction! that destroys all desires,
O Hidden Power! that is the source of all powers,
O Hidden Samrat! who is the King of all kings,

Crores of prostrations unto Thee, O Adorable Lord!
Reveal Thyself unto me now and here.

24. MY CROWN

I CROWN my head with the lotus feet of Lord Krishna
Who with Radha inseparably is blended
Like ice and coolness; fire and heat;
Jessamine and fragrance; life and body;
Diamond and brilliance; form and shadow;
Word and meaning; food and energy;
Who is the doctor for curing the disease of birth and death;
Who feeds His devotees with the nectar of immortality;
Who shelters them in Freedom Mansion;
Who rents asunder the veil of ignorance;
Who burns the five kinds of afflictions;
Who breaks the three old knots;
Who confers immortality and eternal bliss.

25. THE LORD AND HIS SAKTI

THE Lord and His Sakti are inseparably blended
Like flower and fragrance, sun and ray,
Life and body, gem and lustre,
Form and shadow, word and meaning,
Ice and coolness, fire and heat;
Sakti is the Mother aspect of the Lord.
She is the energy aspect of Ishwar.
Siva and Parvati, Vishnu and Lakshmi,
Radha and Krishna, Sita and Rama,
Brahma and Saraswati, Subrahmanya and Valli,
Are one and the same.
Sakti is Sat-chit-ananda Rupini,
Chinmaya Rupini, Anandamaya Rupini.
Obtain the Grace of the Mother.
She will introduce you to Sadasiva,
The Indweller in Sahasrara.

26. DO GRANT THIS PRAYER, O SIVA!

O Lord Siva, Consort of Uma,
O Saranagatha Vatsala,
O Bhakta Vatsala,
I have not served Thee in the past,
Please do save me in spite of it;
I am guilty,
Because I have forgotten Thee.

I have no burning Mumukshutva
Due to weak Samskaras.
Let this body fall down
In full divine ecstasy
In the singing of Thy Name,
Do grant this prayer, O Mahadev!

Sivananda thus sacrifices his soul
At the lotus feet of Neelakantha,
The destroyer of cupid,
The Redeemer of the fallen,
The Indweller of all beings,
Om Namah Sivaya.

27. THE ABODE OF SILENCE

Where there is neither hunger nor thirst,
Where there is neither doubt nor delusion,
Where there is neither pain nor sorrow,
Where there is neither day nor night,
Where there is neither fear nor illusion,
Where there is neither two nor three,
Where there is neither riot nor bomb-throwing,
Where there is neither Pakistan nor Hindustan,
Where there is neither difference nor separation,
Where there are unity, peace and eternal bliss,
Where there are perfection, freedom and independence,
Where there are wisdom and Immortality—

In that supreme abode of silence
Let me ever dwell, my Lord!

28. SIVA'S GRACE

THE LORD who dwells in Mount Kailas,
Who saved Markandeya and Manickavasagar,
Who burnt Cupid when he disturbed His Tapas,
Who gave birth to Skanda to destroy Surapadma,
Who is in the form of twelve Jyotirlingas,
Who gave Pasupatastra to Arjuna,
Who married Parvati the daughter of Himavan,
Who stood as a pillar of light in Arunachal,
Who is the heart of Lord Hari,
Gave me His immaculate feet
And admitted me into His Grace.
My adorations and salutations to Lord Siva!

29. I SAW HIM

I SAW the Lord, Arjuna's Charioteer,
With golden feet like lotus red.
I drank nectar to my heart's content.
I dance in blissful ecstasy;
He also joined me.
What a blessed state!
I sang His praise and glory.
He blessed me.
My bonds slipped off.
All ties were rent asunder.
Om Namo Bhagavate Vaasudeveya!

Chapter IX

HEALTH, HYGIENE AND DIET

1. BODY-TEMPLE

THIS body is a temple of God:
The Lord is the Proprietor of this temple;
He is the Indweller.
It is an instrument for God-realisation,
Therefore it should be kept healthy and strong.
It is a wonderful engine—
The digestion of food, the pumping of blood,
The secretion and excretion,
The functions of brain, liver, heart,
Kidneys and lungs are marvellous.
Food supplies materials
For growth, maintenance and repair,
Food supplies energy and heat;—
The proteins are the tissue builders,
The Prana builds the tissues,
Vitamins are the life-giving substances,
Carbohydrates and fats generate energy,
Minerals are body-building materials.

2. SONG OF VIBHUTI YOGA

(Thars: Sunaja)

BHAJO Radhe Krishna
Bhajo Radhe Shyama

I am spinach among leafy vegetables,
I am almond among all nuts,

Milk am I among perfect foods,
Tomatoes am I among all vegetables;
I am potatoes among tubers and roots,
I am Basmati rice among all cereals,
Soya bean am I among all pulses,
Cow's ghee am I among all fats;
I am mango among all kinds of fruits—
I am 'Alphanso,' among all mangoes,
Buttermilk am I among all beverages,
Glucose am I among all sugars;
I am phosphorus among all minerals,
I am vitamin C among all vitamins,
Lady's finger am I among green vegetables,
Barley water am I among invalid foods;
I am first class protein in milk among all proteins,
I am white sugar among carbohydrates,
Turnip am I among English vegetables,
Lemon juice am I among anti scorbutics.

3. STORY OF VITAMINS

"A"

I AM Vitamin A, enemy of germs.
I live in milk, butter and curd.
I keep the skin healthy.
I remove night blindness.
If you miss me in your food,
I will give you bad eyesight.
I am needed for growth and repair of body.
Take your Vitamin A, my dear;
I will make your skin beautiful.
I will give you good eyesight.
Nursing mothers need me more
To keep their children healthy and strong.

HEALTH, HYGIENE AND DIET

Goodbye friends! Be cheerful!
I shall meet you again on the dining table.

"B"

I am Vitamin B, foe of "Beri-beri".
I belong to a complex group,
B_2, B_3, B_4, B_5, B_6, (H) are my brothers.
Do not cook me with soda.
I will run away immediately.
I am abundant in Marmite and bran.
I had my abode in the paddy:
When people crushed me in the mill,
I left my original home at once.
I am growth promoting.
I make the food extremely palatable.
I am essential for your health and well-being.
Do not miss me, comrade
Take your Vitamin "B".
I shall keep you healthy and strong.

"B_2 or G"

I am Vitamin B_2 or G, enemy of Pellagra.
I am P P 1 Pellagra Preventive.
I am abundant in milk, cereals and pulses.
I am essential to growth and general well-being.
If you miss me in your food,
You will get Pellagra.
I will produce soreness of the mouth.
I am not present in raw milled rice and maize.
If you miss me on your dining table,
I will generate Pellagra.
Take a balanced diet, my child.
Take milk, spinach and curd.
There will be no B_2 deficiency;
You will be robust and healthy.

"C"

I am the foe of Scurvy.
I attack the sailors, and those who do not take vegetables.
I am abundant in orange juice,
Lemon juice and tomato juice.
If you miss me in your food,
I will make your gums bleed.
I enrich the blood.
If you cannot get lemon or orange,
Take Amla or Nellikai!
I am very rich in this fruit.
Make Amla Morabba and take it daily.

"D"

I am the enemy of rickets
And Osteomalaca,
I am present in milk and butter.
I am "Egosterol" and "Calciferol".
I build the bones.
I make use of Calcium and Phosphorous.
I will supply you Vitamin "D",
If you take the sunbath.
I make your teeth strong and healthy,
If you expose your skin and food
To ultra-violet light:
There I am in abundance.

"E"

I am the foe of Sterility.
O Sterile man, O barren woman!
Do not be afraid any more.
I shall remove your barrenness.
You will get healthy children.
Think of me and dance in joy.
You need not go to Rameshwar,

HEALTH, HYGIENE AND DIET

And do Sarpa Santi.
You need not repeat Santana Mantra.
I am abundant in wheat germs,
Lettuce and whole-meal bread.
Take them freely;
I shall make you fertile.

4. HEALTH MENU

HAVE a restricted diet on Sunday
Take an all-fruit diet on Monday
Live on full milk diet on Tuesday
Have the fruit and milk diet on Wednesday
Have full fast on Thursday, the Guru's day
Take all vegetable diet on Friday
Have partial fast on Saturday,
Take milk and fruits only at night.

If you stick to the above dietetic regimen,
Diseases will take to their heals;
You will possess good health and strength,
You will attain longevity;
This will aid you in attaining concentration,
You will have very good meditation,
Try this, follow this and realise the results.

5. FRUITS HIDE THE ATMA

FRUITS, vegetables, proteins and vitamins
Hide "Atma", the Indweller in all objects;
They all dissolve in Atma or the Soul,
They are all Maya's jugglery products.
Fruits etc., are not apart from Atma:
They have no independent existence,
They are superimposed on Atma.
If you behold the Atma,
The fruits etc., will vanish;
If you see the fruits alone,
You cannot see the Atma.

Fruits etc., are projected
Through the illusory power of Atma;
Fruits etc., are mere appearances like mirage.
Atma alone is the only Reality:
Realise this Atma through meditation,
And eat this most delicious Immortal Fruit.

Chapter X

VEDANTIC MEDITATIONS

1. WHO AM I?

SIT calmly and enquire 'who am I?'
This will solve all life's problems,
This will give you freedom and Immortality,
This will destroy all pain and sorrows.

This body of flesh and bone am I not,
It is inert, perishable, with parts,
The senses, eye, ear, nose am I not,
They are finite products of elements.

The five vital airs am I not,
They are inert products of Rajas,
The doubting mind am I not,
It is also inert, finite and perishable.

Satchidananda Brahman am I,
Nitya Mukta Suddha Buddha Brahman am I,
Nirakara, Nirguna, Nirvisesha Brahman am I,
Akhanda Pari Poorna, Vyapaka Brahman am I.

Sword and weapons cut me not,
Fire and atomic bombs burn me not,
Water and deluge wet me not,
Cyclone and wind dry me not.

Vedas, Bible, Koran, Avesta have sung of me,
Rishis, sages and Yogis meditate on Me,
Fire, wind carry out My commands,
Intellect, senses, sun, get light from Me.

Infinite eternal, immortal soul am I,
All blissful, self-contained Atman am I,
All-pervading, self-luminous Purusha am I,
Birthless, deathless, Timeless, Brahman am I.

Unaffected, actionless, silent witness am I,
Source of Vedas, womb, substratum of this world am I,
Inner Ruler, Indweller, homogeneous Essence am I,
King of all Devas, Progenitor of Hiranyagarbha am I.

2. HOW FREE AM I!

O FREE, O gloriously free,
Am I in freedom from birth and death,
From pain, sorrow, Karma and nescience,
All that dragged me back is rent asunder.

How free am I,
How thoroughly free from cares and anxieties,
It is the grace of the Lord,
I am purged now of all impurities,
I dwell in the abode of silence,
Nothing can disturb or distract me.

I have won, I have won,
The wave of bliss sweeps over me now,
The breath of freedom sweeps over me now,
Nityamukta Svaroopoham,
I am eternally free Rasa or essence.

No bending, no kneeling,
No 'good morning sir'
No 'ji huzur sir'
No 'obedient servant'
No 'I beg to remain'

But I am Emperor of the three worlds,
Atma Samrat, Svarat, Self-king.

Suddhoham, Buddhoham, Niranjanoham,
Samsara Maya Parivarjitoham.

Pure, fully illumined, spotless,
Free from the taints of Samsara am I.

3. I AM THE ALL—I

I GIVE power to the vitamins.
I am the stimulant in coffee and tea.
I am nutrition in foodstuffs.
I am the intoxicant in liquors and opium.
I am the attraction in woman,
Gold, dollars, notes and cheques.
I am the celestial manna in heaven.
I am the essence in vaccine injections.
I am the healing agent in all the "Pathies".
I am the power in Atom Bombs.
I am the strength of all Ministers and Dictators.
I am the power in non-violence and truthfulness.
I am the nectar in Sahasrara.
I am sound, language, OM and Vedas.
I am the universe, elements and Devas.
I am the goal, centre and ideal.

4. I AM THE ALL—II

I AM the all, I am all in all,
There is nothing besides my Self.
I am the Soul of the universe, Visva Atma.
I am the Self of all beings, Antaratma.
I am the warp and woof of all.
I alone really exist.
I am here; I am there.
I am now, I was, I will be for ever.
There is neither distance nor space in me.
I am the ocean of existence.
This world is a mere bubble in me.
A drop fell from me
And it became the universe.
My effulgence shines in the form of Brahma,

Vishnu, Siva, Devi, Vyasa and other Rishis.
My essential nature is amazingly wonderful.

5. I AM NIRMALA BRAHMAN

I AM the Satya-Jnana Ananta Brahman.
I am the Nishprapancha, Nirsamsara Brahman.
I am Nitya-nishkala Brahman.
I am Akhanda-Paripoorana Brahman.
I am Sadananda Brahman.
I am Nirmala, Niranjana Brahman.
I am the Brahman without caste, creed.
I am the beginningless, endless Brahman.
I am the Brahman without differences.
I am the diseaseless, decayless Brahman.
I am the Brahman without "this", "that", "I", "he", "you".
I am Amala, Asanga, Nischala Brahman.

6. I AM VIJNANA GHANA BRAHMAN

I AM Atyanta Achala Brahman.
I am Atyanta Sasvata Brahman.
I am Kevala Satmatra Brahman.
I am Kevala Chinmatra Brahman.
I am Kevala Sadananda Brahman.
I am Sankalpa-vikalpa-rahita Brahman.
I am nameless, formless Brahman.
I am Vijnanaghana Brahman.
I am Vilakshana Sarva-adhisthana Brahman.
I am Paricchedarahita Brahman.
I am Svayamjyoti Brahman.
I am Dvandva Ahambhava-rahita Brahman.
I am Duhkha-soka-rahita Brahman.

7. I AM SVATANTRA BRAHMAN

I AM Chaitanyamatra Brahman.
I am Niramaya Brahman.
I am Niratisayananda Brahman.

I am Svatantra Brahman.
I am self existent Brahman (Svayambhu).
I am Aparicchinna Brahman.
I am Avyaya Ananta Brahman.
I am Suddha Vijnana Vigraha Brahman.
I am Tat Pada Lakshya Brahman.
I am Tvam Pada Lakshya Brahman.
I am Nirbhaya Brahman.
I am Akshara Brahman.

8. I AM OMKARA SVAROOPA

I AM that Para Brahma Svaroopa,
Where there is neither ignorance nor knowledge,
Where there is neither honour nor dishonour,
Where there is neither support nor the supported,
Where there are no limiting adjuncts of body, mind, etc.

I am the pure Chaitanya,
Where there is neither bondage nor liberation!
I am the Absolute which the pure mind meditates upon!
I am Omkara Svaroopa—of the essence of OM!

9. I AM NIRAVARANA BRAHMA SVAROOPA

I AM Advaita Para Brahma Svaroopa,
Which is beyond the reach of mind and speech.
I am the pure Satchidananda Brahman,
Where there is neither Subha nor Asubha,
Where there is neither sky nor air,
Neither fire nor water.
I am the pure Brahma Svaroopa,
Where there are neither Sankalpas nor Vasanas,
Where there is neither Vikshepa nor Avarana.
I am Satya-jnana-ananda Svaroopa,
Which is Sakshi for the whole world.
I am Chinmatra Svaroopa,
Where there are neither senses nor mind,

Where there is neither Drishya,
Nor the Triputi of Seer, Sight and Seen.

10. I AM PARABRAHMA SVAROOPA

I AM Para Brahma Svaroopa (the Absolute) without special attributes;
I am the Essence which all the Vedantic scriptures investigate;
I am Anandaghana, embodiment of Bliss;
I am the fruit of Maha Mauna—the Great Silence;
I am the Svaroopa wherein there are neither dualities nor opposites;
I am that Para Brahman wherein there is neither pleasure nor pain;
I am the Absolute wherein there is neither darkness nor light;
I am the Pure Consciousness which cuts the knots of the heart!

11. I AM SATYA SVAROOPA

I AM Satya Svaroopa.
I am Santa Svaroopa.
I am Suddha Sukshma Svaroopa.
I am Vijnana Svaroopa.
I am Nirvikara Svaroopa.
I am Akhanda Ekarasa Svaroopa.
I am Poorna Svaroopa.
I am Nivritti, Sannyasa Svaroopa.
I am Prajnana Ghana Svaroopa.
I am Nitya Chaitanya Svaroopa.
I am Nitya Tripti Svaroopa.
I am Mukti Svaroopa.
I am Santi Svaroopa.
I am Satchidananda Svaroopa.

12. I AM CHAITANYA SVAROOPA

I AM the Truth, the only living Presence!
I am the Svaroopa—essence—which is
                greater than the greatest!
I am the One Homogeneous Essence without distinctions!
I am Akhanda-ekarasa Svaroopa—One Indivisible
                Homogeneous Essence!
I am the Absolute which is beyond the reach of the Srutis!
I am Brahma Svaroopa without motion!
I am That which transcends everything!
I am Chaitanya Svaroopa without the six modifications!

13. I AM CHINMATRA SVAROOPA

I AM Brahma Svaroopa, without the five sheaths!
I am the Absolute Consciousness which is
                within that within!
I am Brahma Svaroopa, without time, space and cause!
I am Chinmatra Svaroopa, which is the essence of
                Wisdom alone!
I am taintless Chinmaya Svaroopa, full of
                Consciousness; where there is "NO"!
I am Poorna Para Brahma Svaroopa which the
                Akhandakara-Vritti is illuminating!
I am Pure Consciousness which has neither
                cause nor effect!

14. I AM SUKHA GHANA SVAROOPA

I AM the Brahman that moves the mind,
I am the Absolute without this world of names and forms.
I am the Eternity where there is no time.
I am the pure Brahman where there is
Neither egoism nor the formidable lust.
I am the Brahman which transcends Gunas,
Which is beyond Sat and Asat.
I am the ever-steady "Sukha Ghana Svaroopa",

I am the Svaroopa where there is
Neither coming nor going,
Neither waking nor dreaming,
Where there is no space to move about,
Where there is Supreme Peace for ever,
Which fills all space everywhere.

15. I AM ANANDA GHANA SVAROOPA

I AM a Kevala Para Brahma Svaroopa,
Where there is neither two nor three,
Where there are neither parts nor divisions,
Where there is neither counting nor measuring;
I am Akhanda Chidakasa Ananda Ghana Svaroopa.
I am Nishkala, Nirdvandva Svaroopa.
I am Niramaya, Nishkriya Svaroopa.
I am Nirakara, Niravayava Svaroopa.

Chapter XI

EXPERIENCES

1. SPIRITUAL EXPERIENCES—I

MORE and more dispassion and discrimination,
More and more yearning for liberation,
Peace, cheerfulness, contentment,
Fearlessness, unruffled state of mind,
Lustre in the eyes, good smell from the body,
Beautiful complexion, sweet, powerful voice,
Passing of little urine and excretion,
Wonderful health, vim, vigour and vitality,
Freedom from disease, laziness and depression,
Lightness of body, alertness of mind,
Powerful Jatharagni or digestive fire,
Eagerness to sit and meditate for long time,
Aversion to worldly talks and company of worldlings,
Feeling of presence of God everywhere,
Love for all creatures,
Feeling that all forms are of the Lord,
That the world is Lord Himself,
Absence of Ghrina or dislike to any creature,
Even to those who despise and insult you,
Strength of mind to bear insult and injury,
To meet dangers and calamities,
Are some of the preliminary spiritual experiences.
These indicate that you are steadily advancing
In the spiritual path.

2. SPIRITUAL EXPERIENCES—II

BALLS of white lights, coloured lights,
Sun, stars, during meditation,
Divya Gandha, Divya taste,
Vision of the Lord in the dream,
Extra-ordinary, super-human experiences,
Vision of the Lord in the human form,
Sometimes in the form of a Brahmin,
Old men, leper, outcaste in rags,
Talking to the Lord,
Are the preliminary spiritual experiences.
Then comes cosmic consciousness or Savikalpa Samadhi,
Which Arjuna experienced.
Eventually the aspirant enters
Into Nirvikalpa Samadhi,
Wherein there is neither seer nor seen,
Wherein one sees nothing, hears nothing,
He becomes one with the Eternal.

3. I DRINK THE NECTAR

MY SADGURU gave me a sword of wisdom.
He united me with the absolute.
He showed me the way to wipe my Karmas.
He removed many pitfalls and snares.
I realised the Supreme State of Changeless Joy,
Wherein the seer, seen and sight are lost.
I live in perfection everywhere.
I have nothing more to learn.
The disease of birth has left me.
I lost myself and became the mass of bliss.
I drink the nectar of immortality,
Which is sweeter than all syrups.'

4. SPEECHLESS ZONE

IN THE perfect nameless, formless Void,
In the unlimited expanse of bliss,
In the region of matterless, mindless joy,
In the realm of timeless, spaceless, stillness,
In the Infinite Zone of speechless, thoughtless peace,
In the transcendental abode of sweet Harmony,
I united with the Supreme Effulgence.
The thought that we are one or two vanished.
I crossed the sea of birth for ever.
This is all due to the Grace of the Lord,
Who danced in Brindavan with rhythmic jingle,
Who raised Govardhan as umbrella for the cowherds.

5. THAT EXALTED STATE

I SEARCHED God in the caves of the Himalayas,
In the pilgrim-centers, in river banks.
But I myself am Brahman, God of gods now!
I had once intense love for my sweet home;
Native village, district, and Province.
But I am now the home of all worlds,
East and West, North and South,
Greece and India, Australia and France,
China and Russia have become one.
I loved Tamil once;
But I am "OM" now,
The source of all languages.
I had once great love for my body;
But now I have realised "All bodies are mine";
Once one hundred years was too big for me;
But I now abide in Eternity;
No time-piece, no calendar is necessary now.
Once five thousand miles was a great distance for me.
But now I feel "I am Infinity".
Time, space have vanished.
I have neither home nor house address nor name!

6. I LIVE IN SILENCE!

THE world may call me good or abuse me.
I do not care now for criticism of the world.
Why should I? When my abode is transcendental!
I am now above good and evil; censure and praise.
I have no connection with body and mind.
I have neither hope, nor fear.
What have I to do with this world?
I am now swimming in the ocean of Brahmic Bliss.
I do not want anybody's favour or recommendation.
I do not wish to interview anybody.
I care not for anybody's company or help.
I live in Silence, enjoy silence, I am silence!
Chelas! Chelees!! And all!!!
Friends! Leave me now please!
Goodbye!

7. BLISSFUL AM I NOW

HOME have I left; the world have I abandoned.
All my mundane desires I have relinquished.
The shallow, hollow nature of this world I have understood.
The worthlessness of all objects I realised.
Lust I have left, anger, pride I have given up.
Craving, longing for objects I overpowered.
I sat on the banks of the Ganga in the Himalayas.
I reflected and contemplated deeply on Brahman,
Ignorance vanished;
My heart is healed.
All Trishnas were ousted from my heart.
All within is purity and peace,
Serene am I now; knowing the peace of the Eternal;
Blissful am I now, realising my essential nature.

8. MY HEART IS BRIMFUL OF JOY!

THE three heart-knots are cut;
All ties have been severed.
All bonds have been broken.
The three fires have been extinguished.
The five afflictions have been burnt.
Old ignorance has vanished.
Maya is hiding Herself in shame.
Poverty, nescience, disease have disappeared.
I am floating in the ocean of joy.
I am light, bliss, peace and harmony.
I have realised the Bhuma, the Great Bliss.
All darkness has been dispelled.
The world has melted in me.
I am a mass of bliss and wisdom.
My heart is brimful of joy and bliss.

9. WELCOME, DISEASE! WELCOME!!

WELCOME disease! Welcome pain!
Welcome microbes! Welcome death!
Welcome malaria! Welcome pyorrhea!
Welcome cholera! Welcome typhoid!
Welcome appendicitis! Welcome!! Welcome!!!
I am not afraid of you all;
Thou art my own manifestation.
The cataract of illusion has vanished;
I behold the Light and Truth everywhere.
You are all my beloved guests in the body.
Health and disease are two ripples
In the ocean of Bliss of Self.
Pain also is pleasure for me!

10. I AM FULL NOW

I KNOW the secret of Brahma-Vidya.
I have realised my essential nature.

Maya is hiding Herself.
She cannot show me Her face.
She is shy to appear before me.
Where shall I go now,
When I am all-pervading and Infinite?
What shall I desire now?
What shall I take?
What shall I renounce?
What work shall I do now?
What is there to achieve?
What shall I seek?
When I am now an Aptakama,
When I possess the whole,
When all my desires are satisfied
By the experience whole,
When I am full, Poornam;
What shall I read now
When I am a man of Wisdom, Chidghana?
To whom shall I deliver lecture
When I alone exist?

11. THE LITTLE 'I' FUSED!

I SAT alone on a block of stone
On the banks of the Ganga, of Bhagirathi.
Mother Ganga blessed me!
I meditated on OM and its meaning,
The Word that is the symbol of Brahman.
The little personality was lost.
The mortal limit of the Self was loosened;
But there was infinite extension.
I entered into the Nameless beyond.
I realised the quintessential unity of bliss.
No words can describe the thrill of joy,
The magnanimous mystic experience,
The supremest and divinest height of felicity!
The little 'I' fused into the incandescent brilliance.
Two became one now.

It was all Tejomaya Ananda,
One mass of transcendental light Bliss.

12. SAMADHI

I DID Japa of OM.
I chanted OM. I sang OM.
I meditated on OM.
The individuality slowly dissolved.
It faded away into the Infinite Being.
The loss of personality is no extinction.
It is the only true, whole, eternal life.
It is the Bhuma experience.
This exalted state is utterly beyond words.
It is not a confused state.
It is a state of ineffable bliss and joy.
It is the clearest of the clearest.
It is the surest of the surest.
It is like the apple in the palm of the hand.
Death here is a ridiculous impossibility.
Immortal elixir flows here perennially.
Wisdom shines in profound effulgence.
Perfect peace reigns supreme!

13. I HAVE BECOME THAT

THE Maya-made world has vanished now!
Mind has totally perished.
The ego has been entirely powdered.
The watertight compartments have been broken down.
Names and forms have disappeared.
All distinctions and differences have melted.
Old Jivahood has entirely fused;
The flood of Truth, Wisdom and Bliss
Has entered everywhere in abundance.
Brahman alone shines everywhere,
One homogenous joy-essence pervades everywhere.

I have become That, I have become That!
Sivoham, Sivoham, Sivoham!!

14. I FOUND HIM OUT

I WANDERED, searched
And then I found Him out at last—
In the silence of the mind.
He is the wonder of wonders:
He is the nectar that never satiates,
He is knowledge's End,
He is the great primal Being.
He is the sweet celestial honey
That destroys old age and death,
He is the endless primeval Light,
He is the medicine sweet
That confers Immortality;
I call Him 'a Mass of Sweetness',
I call Him 'the Milk of Wisdom',
I call Him 'the Ocean of Bliss',
I call Him 'the Old Man of the Upanishads',
I call Him 'the Silent Sleeper in the Sea'.

15. MYSTERIOUS EXPERIENCE

BRAHMAN or the Eternal is far sweeter than honey,
Jam, sugar candy, Rasagulla or Laddu.
I meditated on Brahman, the Immutable.
I attained the stage that transcends finite.
True light shone in me.
Avidya or Ignorance vanished in toto.
The doors were totally shut;
The senses were withdrawn;
Breath and mind merged in their source,
I became one with the Supreme Light.
A mysterious experience beyond speech indeed.
Sivoham Sivoham Sivoham Soham;
Sat-Chit-Ananda Svaroopoham.

EXPERIENCES

16. THE GREAT BHUMA EXPERIENCE

I MERGED myself in great unending joy.
I swam in the ocean of immortal bliss.
I floated in the sea of Infinite Peace.
Ego melted, thoughts subsided,
Intellect ceased functioning,
The senses were absorbed.
I remained unawakened to the world.
I saw myself everywhere.
It was a homogeneous experience.
There was neither within nor without;
There was neither "this" nor "that"
There was neither "here" nor "there";
There was neither "he", "you" or "I" or "she";
There was neither time nor space,
There was neither subject nor object;
There was neither knower nor knowable nor knowledge;
There was neither seer nor seen nor sight;
How can one describe this transcendental experience;
Language is finite, words are impotent,
Realise this yourself and be free!

Chapter XII

SANNYASIN, SAINT AND SAGE

1. SANNYASA

TO GIVE up the illusory names and forms
And to rest in the nameless, formless Absolute is Sannyasa.
To abandon attachment to names and forms
And to get attached to Brahman is Sannyasa.
To kill egoism, the root of mundane life
And to merge in the egoless Atman is Sannyasa.
To destroy ignorance, cravings, likes and dislikes
And to rest peacefully in the Soul is Sannyasa.
To give up the vision of plurality
And to behold unity of Self is Sannyasa.
To slay lust, anger and greed,
And to wear the orange robe of wisdom is Sannyasa.
To shave the mind of all its desires
And to hold the staff of Brahma-jnana is Sannyasa.
To slay the idea of separateness and differences
And to drink the Advaita nectar from the Kamandalu
  is Sannyasa!

2. SANNYASI

A SANNYASI is the Father and Mother of this world.
He is a King of kings, Emperor of emperors.
He is the Supreme Guru of Gurus.
He is an embodiment of nectar and bliss,
Wisdom, love, generosity and divine virtues.
He is an object of reverence and worship for all.
All place their heads at his feet.
All come to him for advice in distress.

He is a Cosmic benefactor and friend;
And so he has neither body-guards nor pilot cars.
He moves very freely in all streets and lanes.
He is councillor to Ministers and Dictators.
He is Manu, the framer of Laws.
He is a Jagat Guru, an Adhyatmic hero.
He comforts, serves and guides all.
He is the supreme wealth of a nation or world.
He is the dispeller of ignorance.
He is a beacon-light in the stormy sea of this Samsara.
He prevents many ship-wrecks in the lives of
                                    many human beings.
He makes others like himself.
He raises others to the state of Divinity,
He is Brahman Himself.
All Devas pay their homage to him.

3. WHO IS A SADHU?

HE, who is ever contented
With whatever he gets;
Who ever repeats the Name of Lord
And sings His Glory;
Who is balanced in pleasure and pain,
Gain or loss, censure and praise,
Honour and dishonour, heat and cold;
Who bears insult and injury;
Who does always good to others;
Who is kind, angerless, and desireless,
Who regards gold as clod of earth;
Who regards all women as his mother or Devi;
Who is free from selfishness, lust and greed;
Who beholds the Lord in all forms—
He is a true Sadhu or Saint.
Glory to such a Sadhu!
Adorations and salutations to Sadhus
Who are veritable gods on this earth!

4. WHO IS A SAGE?

A SAGE is balanced in heat and cold,
Censure and praise, honour and dishonour.
He has perfect self-mastery.
He has equanimity under all circumstances.
He unflinchingly adheres to truth and right.
He is courageous, always cheerful.
He has wonderful power of endurance.
He is free from egoism and mine-ness,
Lust, anger, pride, and selfishness.
He is endowed with divine wisdom.
He can clear any kind of doubts.

5. SAINT NARASI

SRI NARASI Saint went to the bazaar
To get ghee for his father's Shraaddha.
He danced in the bazaar
Singing "Jaya Jaya Radhe Govind".
He forgot all about the ghee and Shraaddha.
But Lord Krishna brought all things Himself.
All the Brahmins were fed sumptuously.
Now Narasi came with his tin of ghee
When the ceremony was over.
He was struck with awe and wonder.
He thought that Lord Krishna Himself
Made all the arrangements.
He saluted Him again and again.
He cursed himself for not having His Darshan.
He praised others for having His Darshan.

This instance clearly supports Gita's promise:
"To those men who worship Me alone,
Thinking of no other, to those
Ever harmonious, I bring full security."

Glory to Gita, Glory to Saint Narasi!
Om Namo Bhagavate Vaasudevaya!

6. VYAVAHARA JNANI AND SAMADHI JNANI

IF A SAGE works for Loka-Sangraha,
He is a Vyavahara Jnani.
If a sage is absorbed in Samadhi,
He is a Samadhi Jnani.
Orthodox Vedantins classify Jnanis
Into Vyavahari Jnanis and Samadhi Jnanis.
They say: Vyavahari Jnani experiences pain,
When his finger is cut,
While Samadhi Jnani does not.
How could this be?
A Vyavahari Jnani also
Is always in his Sahaja Avastha.
He is ever resting in his own Svaroopa.
His work is like a child's play.
He has neither Sankalpa nor agency,
Nor identification with the body.
Their Vyavahara Jnani must be, therefore,
One who has theoretical knowledge of Vedanta,
Who has tall talks and gossips on Brahman,
Who has not done any Sadhana,
Who has no direct experience,
Who is a lip-Vedantin or Pseudo-Vedantin,
Who has read a bit of Panchadasi and Vichara Sagar,
And who knows well the Bandhara dates of all Kshettars
And the addresses of Seths in Mumbai and Kolkotta!

Chapter XIII

INDIA AND HER PEOPLE

1. VANDE MATARAM

Thars: Sunaja

AKHANDA Ram Ram, Ananda Ram Ram,
                               Advaita Ram Ram Ram.
Chidghana Ram Ram, Chinmaya Ram Ram,
                               Chidrupa Ram Ram Ram.
Vande Mataram, Vande Mataram, Vande Mataram,
Vande Mataram, Vande Mataram, Vande Mataram.
Prostrations unto thee, Adorations unto thee,
                               O Mother India,
Thou art free now, Thou art free now,
                               Thou art Independent.
Hail Hail Mother, Hail Hail Mother, Hail Hail Mother,
Victory Victory, Victory Victory, Victory unto Thee.
                               (Vande Mataram)

15th August 1947 is a memorable day
The whole India, the whole nature, rejoices heartily.
Glory to Gandhiji, Glory to Leaders,
                               Glory to the sons of Hind.
Jai Hind Jai Hind, Jai Hind Jai Hind, Jai Jai Jai Jai Hind.
                               (Vande Mataram)

2. THE DAWN OF INDIA'S FREEDOM

THERE is Prarabdha for a country too.
India had her bad days,
For more than eight centuries.

She was oppressed by some greedy men;
And yet she served them and made them happy and rich.
She is ever rich, liberal and Catholic.
She nourishes the whole world.
Her resources are inexhaustible.

Her culture and civilisation are unparalleled.
She is the spiritual teacher of the whole world.
Yogis and sages play in Her lap.
India is the land of philosophy and Yoga.
She will ever be the world's Preceptor.
Every nation has its eye on India.

Fifteenth August 1947 witnesses the dawn of Freedom.
It is indeed a red-letter day.
India's National Flag is floating in the sky now.
Hail India, the land of nectar and eternal bliss!
Victory, victory, victory to Glorious India!!
Hail Bharathavarsha! Hail Aryavarta!

3. GLORY TO GREAT MEN OF INDIA

MY SALUTATIONS to the Great Men,
The brilliant luminaries who shine bright
In the firmament of glorious modern India;
Sri Ramakrishna Paramahamsa,
The Holy Saint and Avatar;
Swami Vivekananda and Swami Rama Tirtha,
The mighty religious prophets;
Dr. Rabindranath Tagore,
The reputed poet philosopher;
Bankim Chandra Chatterji, the patriot-novelist;
Swami Dayananda, the founder of Arya Samaj;
Raja Ram Mohan Roy and Justice Ranade,
The prominent social-reformers;
Sir Brajendranath Seal, the mystic-thinker;
Dadabhai Naoroji, Lokamanya Tilak and Gokhaley,
C.R. Das, Pandit Malaviyaji and Motilal Nehru—
The pioneers of Indian Nationalism;

Lala Lajpat Roy, the fiery politician of Punjab;
The Ali Brothers, the leaders of Khilafat Movement;
J.C. Bose and Acharya P.C. Ray;
The well-renowned research-scholars of Science;
Ramanujam, the famous mathematician;
Sir Srinivasa Sastry,
The silver-tongue-statesman.
May their souls rest in Peace!

II

My salutations and adorations to:
Sri Aurobindo, Maharshi Ramana and Swami Ramdas,
The reputed living saint;
The saintly Gandhiji,
The Beloved of Indian Masses;
Subhas Chandra Bose,
The patriot-martyr;
Jawaharlal Nehru, Maulana Azad,
Sardar Patel, Rajagopalachari,
And Babu Rajendra Prasad,
The top-ranking Congress Leaders;
H. E. Mr. Asaf Ali, the first Indian Ambassador to America;
Veer Savarkar and Dr. Shyama Prasad Mukherji,
The well-known leaders of Mahasabha;
Abdul Guffar Khan, the noble leader
Of Khudai-khidmadgar;
Sir S. Radhakrishnan,
The erudite philosopher of the Orient;
Sir C.V. Raman, the Nobel-laureate scientist;
Muhammad Iqbal, the brilliant Urdu-poet of Punjab;
Dr. B.C. Ray and Dr. Rangachari,
The top-ranking leaders of Medicine;
Abanindranath Tagore, the Oriental Artist
And Ravi Varma, the famous portrait-painter.
May Lord bless them all!

4. GLORY TO INDIA'S GREAT WOMEN

MY ADORATIONS to India's great women!
The crest jewels of modern Bharat:
The talented Pandit Vijayalakshmi,
The first Indian Ambassador to Russia;
Rukmini, the late minister of Madras;
Capt. Lakshmi, the heroine of I. N. A.;
Sarojini Naidu, the poet-politician,
The nightingale-orator;
Ammu Swaminathan of Indian Constituent Assembly;
Amrit Kaur, the leader of Indian Women's Association;
Aruna Asaf Ali, the patriot-socialist.
May Lord bless them with
Health, long life, peace and prosperity.

5. HINDUS WAKE UP

UNITE, unite, join, join, O Hindus!
Abandon all petty differences,
Become like Bhishma, Bhima,
Arjuna and Shivaji.
There is an infinite magazine
Of power and wisdom within you;
The blood of famous Rishis and heroes
Runs in your veins:
You can work wonders!
Sing "The Song of Sivoham, Sivoham."
You are the immortal soul,
Care not for this perishable body:
It is a clod of earth.
March boldly, O undaunted heroes!
And wear the laurel of Immortal Glory.
O Rajputs, Stand up!
Gird up your loins!
Become chivalrous;
Your forefathers have done marvellous deeds
Of valour and superhuman strength.

6. COME NOW, MY KRISHNA!

O LORD! You gave definite promise
"Whenever there is unrighteousness,
I will manifest in this world".
Keep up your promise now:
There is great confusion in India,
There is much Adharma in this sacred land,
There is much bloodshed and hatred;
There is no security or safety:
People are running here and there,
Houses are burnt and looted,
Children and women are butchered,
There is severe famine in this country,
There is curfew everywhere.
Om Namo Bhagavate Vaasudevaya.

Chapter XIV

GARLAND OF YOGA

1. MAN IS LIKE A TREE

MAN is like a tree in the forest.
His hairs are the leaves,
His skin is the outer bark.
Just as sap flows from the bark,
So also blood flows from his skin.
His pieces of flesh are underlayers of wood,
The bones are the wood within.
The marrow is like the pith.

2. HEAD-STRONG MAN

MAN is proud of his head-strong nature.
He says "I am a very head-strong man."
To be really head-strong is sticking to resolutions.
Such as "I will speak truth from today.
I will control my anger. I will observe celibacy.
I will get up at 4 a. m. and do meditation.
I will observe full Mauna today. I will fast
And keep vigil on Sivaratri and Vaikuntha Ekadasi.
I will serve my Guru till the end of life."
This is very good;
This indicates his strong will and Sattvic nature.
I met an educated man,
And said "Do not go to Badri or Gangotri now
As you have no money or blanket,
As your health is not good."
He said "I am a head-strong man,
I will surely go now; let me die on the way,

It does not matter much,
I will never hear anybody's words."
This is Tamasic egoism or foolishness:
This is foolish obstinacy or arrogance.
Such a man always quarrels and fights.
He does not possess adaptability.
He never sticks but becomes rolling stone.
His life is a thorough failure.
The world abounds with such "Head-strong men."

3. STORY OF HORSE "EDAKKU"

THERE is a beautiful horse
In the city of Calcutta.
It is robust and well-built,
It is nicely spotted,
It is a reputed horse—
It has won prizes in the race;
It runs swiftly:
It gallops and gallops;
Its name is "Edakku".
But sometimes it stands on its hind legs,
Pushes the tonga backwards—
People are either hurt or killed.

There are some people and some aspirants too
Like this well-known "Edakku";
They are tactful, able and dexterous,
They have all-round development;—
People admire and admire,
Simply glorify and glorify.
Very often they also stand on their hindlegs
And push the tonga with men in the abyss.
Hence, all are afraid of these horses—
They are not at all useful to the world.
O man! Beware of such dangerous human "Edakkus".

4. THREE "POCHUS"

"POMBILLAI Siricha Pochu,
Pohailai Viricha Pochu,
Sadhu Kettal Pochu"—

If a woman smiles and laughs
She is gone;
People will suspect her character.

If you spread out the tobacco leaves in the air,
They are lost;
Their vigour will vanish.

If a Sadhu begins to ask the householder something
He will lose his respect;
They will say "Here is a beggar".

O woman! do not smile, be modest.
O Sadhu! do not beg or ask for anything;
All things will come to you.
Be dispassionate and renounce.

5. CONTAGION

IN A family Rama gets influenza;
Then Krishna catches the infection.
In an Ashram Neelakant keeps the beard;
Then Aiyana also catches the beard-infection.
In another Ashram Banerjee keeps long hair;
Then Ganapathy catches the infection:
He also grows long hair.
Elizabeth keeps bobbed hair;
Then Lakshmi readily catches the infection.

Mind easily imitates and imitates.
Ananth Ram drinks, smokes and gambles;
In his company Govinda Ram also does the same.
One man keeps a cut in the shirt;
Then all begin to follow him.

Spiritual contagion is more infectious.
Siva leads the life of Nivritti;
Then Venkatesa Dasa also follows him.
Satyakama practises Asanas and Pranayama;
Then Narayana also starts the practice.

Live in the company of Sages and Yogis;
You will readily catch the spiritual contagion.
Then you will quickly grow in spirituality.

6. THIS WORLD—A MYSTERIOUS SHOW

SOME Rajas take delight
In having a hospital and zoo for dogs;
In arranging marriages for them!
And in taking these dogs in marriage procession!!
Some take great pleasure
In breeding good horses and making money.
Some train cocks and bulls for fighting.
Some train hawks for flight.
Some are fond of hunting "Shikar".
Some are great cricketers.
Some start cinema studios.
Some revel in harems "three hundred strong";
Some collect specimen of womanhood from each nation!
Some go for pilgrimage to Kailas.
Some start Sanskrit colleges.
Some write books.
Some do Japa and meditation.
This world is a mysterious show of God.
People have different fancies.
They reap the fruits
According to their fancies and deeds.

7. STRANGE RUSSIA

RUSSIA does not want God;
They feel no necessity for God.
The State will provide all comforts.

The State will give tickets for cinema.
There is no necessity for marriage.
Any man can take any woman.
He can keep her for one or two weeks;
And leave the children in any corner.
The State will look after the children.
This is perfect liberty and freedom.
Man is also imitating the stud-bull.
He has come down to the level of a horizontal being!
Woman does not like that people
Call her as the wife of somebody.
She wants to be absolutely independent!
Can this state of affairs give freedom?
Is this real freedom?
Russia will soon repent and weep for her folly.
This is Vipareeta Buddhi or perverted intellect.
Real freedom is in the Atman or Soul.
O Russia! Attain this through self-restraint,
Study of Upanishads, Brahma Sutras,
Enquiry, purity, devotion and meditation.
Abandon Communism, embrace Vedantism.

8. THE WHOLE WORLD IS RESTLESS NOW

NEW Year 1948 has dawned.
Mr. Truman and Mr. Stalin are counting their atom bombs.
They are restless and sleepless.
One is afraid of the other.
Mr. Jinnah has got his Pakistan;
He has not realised his object.
He is very sick and restless.
He wants to fly to England for treatment.
There is no peace in Pakistan.
There is financial collapse.
There are misery and suffering.
He is upset and repents now.
Kashmir is in trouble.
Sri Hari Singh flew and is Avyakta in Jammu.

Muslims are fighting with Muslims;
This is a great wonder.
Praja Mandal peoples are agitating all over.
Indian Union wishes merging of States.
The Rulers of States are in a dialemma.
Hindustan and Pakistan may have a Jujitsu.
The root cause of all this is ignorance
Which manifests as lust for power.
O Lord! Bring peace on this earth now.
The condition is very serious at present.
Establish Universal Love and Brotherhood!

9. EVOLUTION

I WAS a mineral and died;
And became a plant.
I died as a plant;
And became an animal.
I died as an animal;
And became a man:
And now rose to a Sage
With knowledge of the Self,
With Eternal Radiance of Light, and Bliss,
And attained Brahmic Nirvana, or Kaivalya.

This is no impossible ideal or ordeal for you all.
It is your prerogative and birthright.
You lost the paradise only to regain it.
Struggle, exert, evolve quickly, O Hero!
And rest in your Ananda Svaroopa.

10. NEW LIFE IN DESTRUCTION

WHEREVER there is construction,
Wherever there is creation,
There is surely destruction by its side.
Along with birth, there is death.
Destruction is indeed a necessity
In the Divine Play;

In the play of forces of Nature,
Destruction prepares for new construction,
New evolution and regeneration.
The seed is destroyed,
But the sprout comes out.
Therefore, be not afraid of destruction.
In destruction there is new life.

11. SLEEP—NATURE'S REFRESHER

SLEEP is Nature's refresher and comforter.
It is the chief nourisher in Nature's feast.
It is a homogeneous experience.
It is a healing balm for wounded hearts.
It is death of each day's life.
It gives the clue for the existence of blissful Brahman.
It is a help to the study of Advaita Vedanta.
No one will exchange it for any other blessing
The world can bestow.
Man enters his own Self in sleep.
He forgets all his cares and worries.
The nerve-centres become inactive.
The fatigued mind takes rest in Brahman;
It goes back to its source.
Its nature and cause are enveloped in obscurity.

12. ODE TO SLEEP

O SLEEP! O gentle sleep!
O Nidra Sakti!
Thou art Nature's soft nurse,
Restorative, gentle refresher;
You are a soothing balm and tonic
In distress, pain and sorrow.
You take me to Brahman
And bathe me in Bliss:
You recuperate my nerves and brain
And fill them with fresh energy.

To that Devi who is in the form of sleep,
I offer my humble salutations:
"Ya Devi Sarva Bhuteshu Nidra Rupena Samsthita
Namastasyai Namastasyai Namastasyai Namo Namah."

13. EKA SLOKI GITA

ARJUNA became despondent.
Lord Krishna taught him the immortality of soul.
He asked Arjuna to do action without egoism,
To curb the mind through Vairagya and Abhyasa,
To close the gates and meditate on OM,
To consecrate the fruits of actions unto the Lord.
He spoke all about His Vibhutis
And gave Arjuna Visvaroopadarsana.
The Lord said: "A devotee is alike to foe and friend,
Also in fame and disgrace, cold and heat.
Prakriti does everything and Atma is actionless.
Sattva is peace; Rajas is passion; Tamas is darkness.
A Gunateeta is balanced in pleasure and pain.
Maya is Asvattha with roots in Brahman."
The Lord asked Arjuna to develop divine qualities,
To give up Asuric Tapas and take Sattvic food,
And practise the three kinds of Tapas.
He made Arjuna understand what is Tyaga-Sannyasa.
He gave him his last teaching:
"Abandon all duties; come unto Me for shelter;
Sorrow not, I will liberate thee from all sins."
Wherever is Krishna, wherever is Partha,
There are surely Prosperity, Victory,
                    Happiness and Justice!

Chapter XV

SIVA AND HIS ABODE

1. WILL OF SIVA

THE sun may rise in the West;
It may delay in rising.
The Mount Kailas may be shaken by a storm.
The jessamine may give up its aroma.
Ice may abandon its coolness.
Fire may relinquish its heat.
Diamond may give up its lustre.
The Pole Star may change its position.
Savitri may give up her chastity.
But the will of Siva is ever strong and adamant.
It never undergoes waning or agitation.
Never, even by an error, is there a decline in its potency!

2. SIVA THE SOURCE

THIS world is a straw for me.
It has no attraction for me.
It is quite valueless for me.
I am the Infinite Ocean of Consciousness.
Countless worlds rise and fall in me.
My effulgence is ablaze
In the sun and the moon.
My beauty is shining in all women,
Charming scenery, landscapes,
Flowers, rainbow and Himalayan snow-clad peaks.
See! Siva is everywhere.
He is the home of all worlds.
He is the source for light, wisdom and beauty.

3. MINE IS THE SOVEREIGNTY SUPREME

HIRANYAGARBHA is born of me.
Indra, Varuna and Yama are my attendants.
They carry out my commands.
Maya is my power.
The seven Rishis are my messengers.
The Guardians of the Quarters
Are my gate-keepers.
I am the Ruler of the three worlds.
O all Emperors, Kings and Cabinet.
My dominion is limitless.
My treasury is inexhaustible.
Kubera is my treasurer.
Vayu moves my Cosmic Punka.
Varuna waters the main roads.
Agni sweeps my verandah.
Surya superintends the power-house.
Parjanya looks after the garden.
Mine is the Sovereignty Supreme.

4. MY MINISTERS

HERE are Ministers of A.K. Government.
Kubera is my Finance Minister:
Even if there is no money,
He arranges for decoration in the Viswanath Mandir
And feeding of Sadhus and the poor on the Pratishtha Day.
Annapoorna is my Food Minister:
She arranges for the foodstuffs;
Somehow they come at the right moment.
Thousands are sumptuously fed.
Aswani Kumars are my Health Ministers:
They take charge of the Charitable Hospitable.
Brihaspati is my Education Minister.
Karma Yogi Hanuman is my Work Minister:
He sends good workers from time to time;
All works are somehow going on efficiently.

Viswakarma is my Construction Minister:
He sends Engineers at the right moment.
My salutations and adorations to these
                              celestial Ministers!

5. MY TREASURY SERVES ME WELL

I WANTED Rs. 10 for Laddu Prasad yesterday;
It as "No"
But my treasury served me well.
I sent Daulat Ram at once and got it.
I wanted Rs. 25 for Swami Swaroopanandaji's railway fare;
It was "No".
But my treasury served me well.
I gave him at once and sent him to Parsa.
The balance of my treasury is Rs. 65 now.
It will be ever full;
And serves me at all times.

A cart will run very smoothly
If the two bulls work in unison.
The Society will run harmoniously
If all work with joined hands.
All Ministers should co-operate;
Then alone will the Cabinet work efficiently.
O Sweet Harmony! Dwell in the hearts of all workers,
O Peace! Pervade and permeate all hearts.
O Dictators, O Premiers, O Secretaries,
Unite, co-operate, enquire, know the source,
Disseminate Peace, stop all conflicts.

6. MY SWEET ABODE

I AM the tongue of Kalidasa,
The head of Sri Sankara;
I am the hand of Raja Janaka;
The eye of Arjuna;
I am the heart of Buddha;
The ear of Dattatreya;

I am the face of Cupid;
The body of Vyasa;
I am the ear of Vasishtha,
The breath of Patanjali Maharshi;
I am the feet of Lord Krishna;
The nose of Lord Rama;
I dwell in thy heart:
That is really my abode!

7. MY SADGURU

MY Sadguru tore the veil of ignorance;
He showered his grace on me,
Just as the sun dispels darkness,
So He removed the darkness of nescience.
He initiated me into the mysteries of Brahma Jnana.
He taught me the significance
Of the Great Text—"Tat Tvam Asi" Mahavakya.
He explained to me all about "Pranava Rahasya".
He made me drink the Nectar of Immortality.
Glory to my Sadguru, the Supreme Jnana Jyoti.
Adorations and prostrations unto Him!

8. GOOD BYE, O DEATH!

O DEATH! O Time! O Kaala!
Show me thy face now.
You cannot frighten me at all.
Thyself and thy messengers are my light tiffin!
I welcome you with a sweet smile.
I am Time of time.
I am Death unto Death itself.
Why are you afraid of me now?
If I like I will cast off this mortal coil;
Or I will convert it into Light.
Go thy own way, my sweet friend!
Do thy duties justly and properly.
Kabardar, comrade;

SIVA AND HIS ABODE

Please do not enter the vicinity of Ananda Kutir;
Goodbye, Lord Yama, Farewell friend!

9. GOODBYE

GOODBYE, medicines and drugs, goodbye!
Goodbye, hospital and patients, goodbye!
Goodbye, medicine, surgery, goodbye!
Goodbye, friends and relatives, goodbye!
Goodbye, stethoscope, thermometer, goodbye!
Goodbye, microscope and tests, goodbye!
Goodbye, Malaya and Singapore, goodbye!
Goodbye, O dear Tambraparni, goodbye!
Goodbye, Madras, Pattamadai, Tirunelvely, goodbye!
Goodbye, Rasam, Sambar, goodbye!
Goodbye, coffee, Iddli, Uppuma, Dosai, goodbye!
Goodbye, Tamil, Tamil Nadu, goodbye!

10. SIVA'S MAGIC

IT WAS August 10th, 1947
The Diamond Jubilee Volume had to be printed.
The manuscripts were ready,
Swami Paramanandaji was ever looking at the postman,
The purse and safe were empty.

But Siva performed a magic,
He brought full security,
He kept his word of his Sloka IX-22,
He sent Sri Kasiram Guptaji to do the work.

How gracious and kind He is!!!
Glory to Lord Krishna who is Siva!

The steps to the Mandir had to be constructed,
The Lord again brought "Yoga Kshemam";
He sent the Amritsar devotee to take up the work.

The Viswa Kalyana Yajnashala foundation was laid,
This is a huge work, no "Rupchand"; "no sinews of war"

Again the Lord sent a devotee from the West
And a devotee from Santa Cruz,
To start the work.

O Lord! salutations unto Thee,
Thy ways are mysterious,
Continue your magic and shower Thy grace.

11. TAP THE SOURCE

A GENTLEMAN or a scientist or a Premier
Takes a whiff, or a peg or a "Sthenga",
Then alone begins to work hard, writes and thinks;
But I stroll in the upstairs for a while
That is opposite to Diamond Jubilee Kutir,
Look at the Ganga and the Himalayas,
Chant OM and do a little Bhastrika,
Compose poems and write articles.
Chanting OM fills one with new energy;
Bhastrika renovates and energies.

Tap the source, your own Inner Self,
And draw power, energy, strength and peace,
Rely not on external useless stuff
And entangle yourself in rotten vicious habits,
And waste not money, time and energy.

12. LORD VISWANATH

THE Supreme Light of lights,
Whose head and feet could not be seen
Even by Lord Brahma and Hari,
Who is subtler than the subtlest,
Greater than the greatest,
Who is self-existent, transcendental,
Who is causeless, formless and timeless,
Who is my Prabhu, Paribhu and Swayambhu,
In Viswanath Mandir, Shivanandanagar,
He has His abode this day,

To save the thirsting aspirants.
What a great blessing indeed to the Sadhakas!
My prostrations to Lord Viswanath!

13. INVITATION TO LORD DATTATREYA

O LORD Dattatreya of Girnar Hills,
Oudhumbhar and Ganagapur;
Beloved of Atri and Anasuya,
The forefather of Avadhoota Sannyasins,
Instructor of Avadhoota Gita to Lord Subrahmaya,
Disciple of twenty-four Gurus,
Instructor to King Yadu;—
O Trimurti Avatara!
Salutations unto Thee.

You are now a neighbour of Lord Viswanath;
Sridhar and Venkatesa Dasa are attending on Thee.
They are putting lights and offering flowers.
Please come and stay in Viswanath Mandir permanently;
I will look after Thee with great care;
Please take the Devi with Thee,
I shall offer nice kitchadie:
Brahmananda Swami prepares it with love,
You will like it immensely;
I will not surely give you Rasagulla,
Because you are a Virakta Swami.
Prostrations unto Thee, O Lord, again and again,
Please do come, O Lord,
R.S.V.P. Sivananda, Post Ananda Kutir.

14. KRISHNA, JOIN MY KIRTAN

O KRISHNA! Come quickly,
And join my Kirtan.
It is held daily at Ananda Kutir,
At 7 p.m.,
On the bank of the Holy Ganga;
Many aspirants take part in the Kirtan.

Bring Radha and Gopis also:
Let them also enjoy the Kirtan;
Bring the cow-herd boys too,
Bring also your friend Arjuna.
Teach again the Gita;
I will also be benefited this time.
Bring Narada Rishi also;
Let him play the Vina.

You and Radha can enjoy the Jhula:
I myself will swing Thee—
Salutations unto Thee, O Lord!
OM Namo Bhagavate Vaasudevaya.

15. THE DIVINE LIFE SOCIETY, RISHIKESH

THIS was founded in 1936
To disseminate spiritual knowledge,
Of Vedanta, Raja Yoga and Bhakti,
Karma Yoga and Hatha Yoga.

It has branches all over the world,
And helps aspirants in a practical manner;
The Divine Life Trust Society
Is the parent institution.

He who practises Ahimsa,
Satyam and Brahmacharya
To the best of his ability
Can become a member.

It is an all-embracing institution,
It has no pet dogmas,
It has no secret doctrines,
Its principles are universal.

It conducts Sadhana weeks
During Easter and Christmas.
It has the Sivananda Publication League,
To Preserve the writings of the founder.

The "Divine Life" is its monthly organ in English,
There is a "Membership Supplement" also.

It conducts a free primary school,
A charitable dispensary and a library,
And has the Post office—Ananda Kutir.

It accommodates for Sadhana
Brahmacharis, Grihastis and Vanaprastis,
Sannyasis and Sadhus,
The "Annaksetra" feeds Mahatmas and the poor.

Students are trained in Yoga,
In lectures and service;
In meditation and Pranayama,
In Asanas and Sankirtan.

It gives instructions on Yoga
Through post,
It conducts classes, prayer
And common meditation too.

It distributes free pamphlets
On Yoga, Bhakti and Vedanta;
It has five sections,
Vedantic, Yogic, Bhakti,
Youth section and Ladies section too.

It disseminates knowledge
Through gramophone records, movies
And Magic Lantern slides,
It holds spiritual conferences as well.

16. RULES OF THE SIVANANDA ASHRAM

For Sadhakas

HARI OM! Om Namah Sivaya!

Any one who really wishes to practise Sadhana
Can remain in the Ashram.
He should first see the General Secretary,

He should take part in the Akhanda Kirtan,
He should attend the class at night.

He should be present in the temple,
During morning and evening worship,
He should do at least twenty Maalas of Japa
And study Gita or Ramayana.

He should not smoke.
He should not take self shaving,
He should take care of the things
That are kept in the room.

He should try to practise
The twenty instructions.
He should get up at 4 a.m.
For morning meditation.

He should not give any money
To the servants or the inmates.
He should not waste his time
In chit-chatting or idle gossiping.

He should ever engage himself,
In Sadhana or study
Or some selfless service
In the Ashram.
He should keep spiritual diary,
And write Mantras.

He should do everything himself,
He should not depend on servants,
He should observe discipline and behave well,
He should be self-controlled and moderate.

There is no payment for boarding and lodging
But the Society accepts voluntary donations.

                Om Namo Narayanaya.

APPENDIX

1. GANDHIJI'S DEATH

MAHATMA Gandhi, the Apostle of Non-violence,
Was violently shot down at Delhi.
This is nothing strange;
Many great Saints had such an end.
Lord Jesus was crucified at the Cross.
Lord Krishna was shot by the hunter's arrow.
Mansoor was cut into pieces.
Socrates took the cup of hemlock juice.
Swami Dayananda was also poisoned.
Many Saints were killed and burned in Pakistan.
This is nothing for the Saints,
Because they are above body-consciousness.
In reality they have no body;
They are ever resting in the Lord;
They are one with the Divine,
It is nothing for them;
Whether the body is embalmed and kept in a shrine,
Or the slough is thrown on the dung-hill:
Whether the body is shot or poisoned.
Everybody's Prarabdha is mysterious.
It is only the ignorant men of the world
Who make a lot of fuss and noise.

2. ODE TO MAHATMA GANDHIJI

(Born: 2nd October, 1869; Died: 30th January, 1948)

O ADORABLE Karma Yogi Veer,
The great Father of the Indian Nation!
Prostrations and salutations unto Thee!
Thou art an Apostle of Peace,
Thou art the Father of Satyagraha,

WAVES OF BLISS

Civil disobedience, non-cooperation movement.
Thou art the real friend of the down-trodden,
Thou removed untouchability.

Through thy undaunted work for thirty years,
India has won her independence.
The whole world mourns for thee;
They fast, pray for thy peace.

You wanted to live for 125 years,
But destiny willed it otherwise.
Thou art a soldier philosopher,
A dynamic saintly politician,
Ahimsa is thy creed.

This world has not produced
And will not produce a dynamic saint like thee.
Glory unto thee, O revered Saint!
We all did prayer on the Ganga-bank
And Kirtan in the Bhajan Hall.

May thy soul rest in peace.
It is you who shook the British Government,
Through thy Tapas and soul-force,
You purified thyself through
Countless fasts and "Ram Nam Japa."

You left the mortal coil with "Hey Ram" on thy lips,
And attained the abode of Immortal Bliss,
Thy last conversation with Sri Sardar Patel,
Is treasured in his heart.

Lord Mountbatten, Nehru, Patel,
Sarojini and Maulana are Shedding tears.
You won triumph, through 'Charkha',
Truth, non-violence and purity.
You worked a miracle and brought peace in
                              Kolkata and Delhi.

APPENDIX

Your work will continue with more force,
You will ever live in the hearts of all.
The West and Pakistan also are feeling thy separation,
You have immortalised thy name.
You have done all that you wanted.
You have changed the mentality of millions.
Thou art the embodiment of patience, peace,
And all divine virtues.

Again and again my adorations unto Thee,
Glory, glory to Mahatma Gandhiji,
The Divine child of Bharata Mata in her Gujarati soil.

3. MIRA BEHN

SHE is an angelic woman,
Bapuji transmuted her into divinity,
She is an image or ray of Mahatmaji.

In fact she is a miniature Gandhiji,
She is an embodiment of Bapuji's virtues,
She is also a Karma Yogini.
At 53, now her walking is running.
The young secretary cannot cope with her.

She is developing "Goloka" near Ramnagar,
What a marvellous divine work!
It is highly pleasing to Lord Krishna;
Gopala, the protector of cows.

It will become Uttara Brindavan soon.
Mira is striving her every nerve
In looking after the cows.

Lord Krishna will come again
To tend the cows and play the flute,
And teach Gita once more,
He will bless Mira who is Radha,

Who is modern Sulabha,
And all His devotees.

May Lord bless Mira with health,
Long life, peace, prosperity and Kaivalya.
Glory to Mira and her Bapu, Gandhiji,
The builder of Indian Nation,
Apostle of Peace and Ahimsa.